AS I SEE IT

RALPH P. KARSTEDT

FAIRWAY PRESS

DRAWER L • LIMA, OHIO 45802

AS I SEE IT

Second Printing 1997

FIRST EDITION
Copyright © 1985 by
Ralph P. Karstedt
Galveston, Indiana

7563 / ISBN 0-89536-937-0

Table of Contents

You lay open the thin book's cover and begin to read;
I, also, am moving through these pages; surely we will meet;
For the story is that of life, of yours and of mine,
And we traverse the chapters of experience together.
In a sense the book is not completely written,
For its telling will inevitably be continued through us;
The great saga of life is, I think, never punctuated with a period;
But rather with commas and semicolons which portray its eternal
unendingness.
Laughter and tears shall surely collide within us as we progress
And move towards the chapters that are yet to be written;
Let us pause now to clasp hands and to allow our souls to meet;
We must be friends, for we are co-authors of tomorrow.

INTRODUCTIONS

If I were a cynic, I would tell you that this book was inspired by the after effects of a late night Chinese dinner. The meal was consumed last May while I was making a return trip from an evening hospital visit in Indianapolis. It got to me at about 3:00 a.m., when I woke up to discover that my insides had become a battlefield for the egg rolls and the sweet and sour pork. As the combat continued in my lower regions, I lay awake and allowed my mind to wander. It was during those hours of sleeplessness that these pages were conceived.

If I were a mystic I would insist that this work was inspired by the moving and guiding hand of God. I would declare that the divine purpose is constantly being woven into and drawn out of our experiences. I would tell you that God's merciful grace has conducted me through the various happenings of my life, and that it is surely the inspirational shadow that has evoked these chapters.

If I were a scholar, I would insist that this book is the natural and inevitable result of my life in general and of a recent doctoral study in particular. The study had a very formidable title: *The Impact Of My Physical Blindness Upon My Ministry At The Burlington United Methodist Church.* Although the title is big enough to gag even the most avid of readers, the doctoral paper did contain a number of insights and ideas that simply had to be shared with the general public. Given my background in communications, it was nearly beyond question that I should decide to popularize my ideas of my desert-dry doctoral effort and season them with a number of laugh- and tear-evoking experiences from out of my life.

But I am not a cynic, or a mystic, or a scholar. Let me put it a different way. Perhaps I am all of these, for I am really rather eclectic. Like a cook who tries a little bit of this and a little bit of that; like a golfer who takes the advice of several different pros, each of whom has a different concept of the game; like a traveler who knows that his trip cannot be complete unless he has flown, bussed, driven, sailed, and walked during the course of his wanderings; I am an eclectic. I believe that the Chinese dinner, the Divine spirit, and the accumulated efforts of my life have all had their place in this enterprise. For who is to say that God did not initiate the conflict between the egg roll and the pork, and who can declare that the efforts of my doctoral study were not intended by a greater power to be made popular in some sort of written work? Am I surrendering to mysticism as I write these words? I rather think that I am accepting the interaction of life's many factors and forces. In any event, the time has come for me to stop sounding like a preacher and simply to introduce myself and these pages.

I tell my daughter and my congregation that my real and official title is the Reverend Doctor Ralph P. Karstedt, Sir! Beth tried this marvelous appellation once and broke out laughing. One of my parishioners heard me use it and called me Ralphie when she met me in the restaurant the next day. Actually, I don't care what you call me. Dad isn't as appropriate for you as it is for Beth; Ralph is okay with me. I will myself use lots of names to talk about me as these pages continue.

I was born in Indianapolis in 1935 and grew up in a small-town-like neighborhood on the south side of that city. I am a husband, a father, a United Methodist minister, a once-upon-a-time violinist, a lover of murder mysteries, a biker, a speech teacher, a sports fan, and a whole bunch of other things too. I am going bald, and, most obvious to most people, is the fact that I am blind.

To my memory I never could see out of my right eye. When I recently uncovered a doctor's statement describing my eye conditions, I read that I could see shadowed forms through that eye when I was an infant. If that is so, I simply don't remember it. To my mind, I never could see from the starboard side.

The left eye was something else. Although my vision through it was never good, it got me through the days of my childhood fairly well. I remember reading countless books, rambling about our community on my two-wheeler, playing basketball out behind a neighbor boy's house, and trying to play a bit of softball.

The softball was nearly too much for me. I could handle grounders okay, but when the ball got into the air, I simply couldn't track it. I recall playing second base one day when a high pop fly was sent my direction. I hadn't the faintest notion where it was. I put up my hands to shade my face and was surprised beyond belief when the ball hit them. I hung on to it with a big smile and instantly raised my reputation with the friends who must have liked me a great deal to let me play on their team. They either liked me or else they were desperate for another player; I don't really know which.

In any event, the left eye got me through grade school and into Shortridge High School there in Indianapolis. It took me through my year as a timid freshman and started me out as an all-knowing sophomore. Then, poof! It happened on a Friday afternoon just before a mid-October football game. I discovered that I had a great big cloud of something in my left eye. The cloud swam around in front of me and wouldn't let me see things properly. As I recall it now, I told my folks that I didn't feel very well that evening. I didn't go to the game. For me, by the way, not going to a game was a major concession.

The cloud went away, more or less, in a few days, and I had almost forgotten it until it returned with new oomph a month or so later. At this point, my calendar of memory makes no sense at all. I simply recollect a period of about two and a half years when clouds would come and go and when each one would leave me seeing less than I had been able to see before. The curious thing is that I didn't tell my parents about the condition. I did make one trip to our family eye doctor, who, I believe, phoned a well-loved uncle in Michigan who has had similar visual problems. Neither the doctor nor I spoke to my folks, however. I shudder as I think of this today. If my daughter were to play such a foolish trick as I had done, I would want to hang her up by her heels. Mom and dad didn't catch on for a long time. I think now that they may have wanted not to see what was plainly before them. Anyhow, it was winter of my senior year in high school before things got so bad that I had to confess all and face up to facts along with my folks.

In March of 1953 I experienced a climactic set of gushers (medically known as retinal hemorrhages), and that's the end of the story insofar as Ralph's seeing was concerned. After that time I visited a couple of doctors, and we tried one or two special treatments, but it was all pointless. By then the only really important thing was that I should accept the fact of my blindness and somehow get myself ready for college.

The rest of my personal story will appear in patches in the pages which follow. Let me simply say now that I did make it through college (Butler University, cum laude 1957), through seminary (Christian Theological Seminary, magna cum laude 1961), got a masters degree in 1963, and worked my way through to a Drew University Doctor of Ministry in 1980. I was ordained into the ministry in 1961, married in 1962, became a father in 1966, and am continuing to experience a full and exciting life.

Before going farther, let me take a moment to introduce you to my family. My wife, Mary Evelyn, and I met (would you believe) on a blind date in September of 1961. I'm not kidding when I write this. We each had a married friend who couldn't stand the thought of their acquaintances being single. Our friends got their heads together and pretty soon we were out on a "blind date." We liked and enjoyed each other immediately, and "like" marvelously was transformed into "love." On July 8th of the following year, on the hottest Sunday of the summer, we were married.

Our daughter Beth came on the scene four years later. We had been reluctant to have children of our own, because I was convinced that my blindness was probably hereditary. (Remember my Michigan uncle.) Beth, therefore, was adopted. Seldom has there been a more wanted child. We got the word of her coming late one Tuesday evening. We returned home well after 11:00 p.m. and found that our phone was ringing almost as soon as the house lights came on. A neighbor, whose phone number we had left with the adoption agency, was on the line with the news. She started out by stuttering and saying: "I don't really know how to go about telling someone that they are parents." She had already done a pretty good job.

The next day we drove to Indianapolis and were shown a marvelous little girl. I am still unable to comprehend the apparent idiocy of the social worker who told us: "You don't have to take her, you know," and "Would you like an hour or so to think about it?" Within that hour or so we were already half-way home.

The only remaining member of our immediate family is Mr. French, my faithful poodle who is lying at my feet as I sit and type out these words. He sometimes spends Saturday mornings in my office and snoozes while I prepare my sermons. (Lots of folks will do it on Sunday; why shouldn't he get an early start on the game?) Believe me when I write that Mr. French is the only dogmatic theologian in my study. As I told you earlier, I personally am an eclectic.

Believe it or not, this story is not about me. It is not even intended to be a narration of my experiences. It is, rather, a view of life, a vision of the ways of men and women, as this view has come to me through my unique perspective. Face it, a blind person sees things differently than most people do. Some of the things are plain outright funny. Others are enough to make a guy cry. Still others are simply interesting.

This, then, is the time for introductions to come to an end and for insights to begin. It is a time for you to look at life as I see it.

When the rain comes and brings dampness to the parching soil,
  We give thanks to God, for he has sent life from heaven.
But when that rain continues and becomes increasingly intense,
  And when dampness is replaced by torrential power,
  We cry "too much!" and pray that the storm will cease.
So fine is the line between enough and too much,
  For what seems adequate can quickly become tragic,
  And much of the difference is in the mind of man.
It is the humor and imagination that you and I pack within the
  suitcases of our souls that is the key to the whole matter,
For they can cause the floodtides of despair to be seen as the vehicles
  upon which we are carried into unimagined tomorrows.

It Hurts Too Much To Cry

When, in November of 1956, Adlai Stevenson was defeated at his second run at the presidency, the time came for the conquered candidate to face the nation and the press. Mr. Stevenson stood on the front porch of his Illinois home and joked with the many reporters who swarmed about him. Finally, one of the newsmen raised the question, "Mr. Stevenson, how can you laugh at a time such as this?"

The indomitable Adlai immediately replied, "I have to laugh; it hurts too much to cry."

That quotation has remained in my mind ever since I first heard it through our living room TV speaker. I have since been told that it may have been originated by Abe Lincoln nearly a century earlier. I have heard it attributed to other persons, too. Frankly, I don't really care who spoke it first. The statement carries the impact of truth. There is indeed a time when a person must laugh because "it hurts too much to cry."

I have learned to laugh a great deal about my blindness. Some of my friends have told me that I may be laughing too much and that I may be using the mask of humor to disguise a horrendous amount of hurt within me. Perhaps they are right. I am sure that I do have hurts and that there have been times when I have attempted to heal them with the ointment of laughter. I am equally sure that my blindness has enabled me to view life from a perspective that can only be described with the words "absurd" and "funny." I see such humor in myself; I see it in people like you; and I even see it through the experiences that you, and others like you, have related to me. Let's face it, there may be times when it does hurt too much to cry. It is also a great deal more fun to laugh. Would you care to join me?

As I write these pages, I am remembering an experience that I had in a lovely Indianapolis home many years ago. I was attending an afternoon tea in this beautiful north-side residence. I hope that you have been noticing some of the adjectives that I have employed in this moment of description. "Lovely," "beautiful," "north-side," "tea" — consider the words again and perhaps you will get the idea. I was taking part in an elegant and posh affair.

In any event, I was sitting in the den of that beautiful home enjoying a high calorie conversation with a very close friend. We were side by side on a divan, and a table laden with goodies was just a couple of feet in front of us. We would talk, and, from time to time, one of us would rise, take a step over to the table, and load up with more goodies.

There came a break in the conversation, and I heard a footstep moving up to the table. In a flash of insight I knew that my moment to strike had come. I always have been a bit of a dog at heart, and I couldn't contain myself as I suddenly sensed the chance to have a bit of fun with my friend. I spoke out just loudly enough that I was sure every one else in the room could hear. "You pig; can't you do anything but eat?"

There was a sudden hush. Then I felt my friend's elbow punching me in the side. A moment later I discovered that it was our hostess who had stepped up to our table.

Do you begin to get the idea? You have to laugh; it hurts too much to cry.

There is one thing that you can say about me as a preacher. No one has ever accused me of reading my sermons. I have long since developed a style of preaching that leaves me totally free from manuscript and notes. It involves mental outlining and out loud rehearsal. This style enables me to stand up and talk with folks. I am totally convinced that my congregations love it. After all, most folks would rather be spoken to than read at.

There are absolutely no sour grapes in this insistence that my spoken style of speaking is, in my judgment, the best way for any preacher to go. If I were to get my sight back today, I would continue to speak without manuscript and notes next Sunday. As a matter of fact, I am developing a growing desire to teach a seminary course in this style of preaching. I would that more pastors had the ability and skill to stand up and talk with their congregations.

If I don't read sermons, it is also true that I have never been accused of reading the various liturgies of the church. I have long since committed to memory the significant rituals for marriage, for baptism, for the reception of members, and for the burial of the dead.

Parishioners tell me that they appreciate the personal quality that such memorization enables. A bride and groom, for instance, don't really like to have a book stuck between them and the minister officiating at their wedding. To put the matter differently, that couple really likes the closeness of a pastor being able to communicate directly with them as they stand at the altar of their church. My system works beautifully . . . well, at least most of the time.

Right now I am thinking of a wedding that I conducted in a small town church near Marion, Indiana. As I recall, it was a Saturday evening event that must have been in the late winter. I know that the sanctuary was dark enough for candle light to have a striking effect. The candles were in all the windows as well as down the main aisles of the church.

The time had come for the wedding to begin. The organ had played, the groomsmen, all spiffed out in their tuxes, were at the front of the sanctuary. The beautiful bridesmaids were all in their places, and the bride had triumphantly entered the church with hand upon her daddy's arm. A hush fell upon the gathering as all waited for me to begin.

Let me now pause to tell you that I use the very traditional United Methodist wedding ritual. It commences with the words: "Dearly beloved, we are gathered together here in the sight of God and in the presence of these witnesses to join together this man and this woman . . ." The ceremony goes on. I am sure that you have heard it half a hundred times.

May I also tell you that when I preside at a funeral I begin the service with these words: "Dear friends, we are gathered together this afternoon to give Christian burial to the body of our departed friend and loved one . . ." I go on to name the deceased.

Have you already gotten the idea? Somehow, some way, Karstedt's computer flipped a chip and started working on the wrong program. There in that hushed sanctuary, standing before 200 guests and a lovely young couple, I began to say: "Dear friends, we have come together to give Christian b . . ." I caught myself in that last split second. No one, except my poor wife who was about to have a heart attack, realized what was taking place. I stuttered for a moment and then plunged on. "We have come together this evening to give Christian b . . . Christian marriage to this man and woman." It was smooth sailing from then on, but wow!

I have positive proof that this ingloriously started wedding actually took place. There is a tape recording of the event. I have told the story about it very often, but from that day to this I have never disclosed the name of the couple in question. Those kids never have known how close they came to being buried instead of married.

I wrote a moment ago that I have never been accused of reading a sermon. I stand by the truth of that statement. I must admit, though, that a few folks have asked me if I ever use pulpit notes that are made out in Braille. To this question I give a hearty "No" response.

I confess to knowing only a little Braille. I can make my way through the patterns of dots enough to enjoy an evening card game with my Braille-marked cards, or to challenge my wife with a couple hours of Scrabble with my game's Braille marked tiles. Once in a long time I use my Braille stylus to note a phone number that I wish to carry with me in a shirt or jacket pocket. Basically, however, I am not a reader of Braille.

Perhaps I should explain that the U.S. government has a superb program that goes by the name of Talking Book Service. It provides recorded books on either tape or discs to any person who cannot see well enough to read ordinary print. This Talking Book program is so excellent that I simply haven't had the need to develop a skill in finger reading.

All of this Braille discussion reminds me of a conversation on a May evening in 1958. At that time I was finishing my first year in seminary and was serving as a youth minister at my home church in northside Indianapolis. On the evening in question our church's young people had gathered around the kitchen table to drink Pepsi, munch pop corn, and talk. The conversation drifted into the subject that is dear to the heart of every high schooler in the merry month of May. No, I am not speaking of romance, I am talking about tests. Finals were coming. It was all the kids could talk about.

After the talk had made two or three turns about the table, I decided that I would have to get into the act. I told the kids that I had the perfect system. "Look," I said, "all I have to do is to make crib notes on small cards in Braille and then drop those cards into my jacket pocket. There isn't a teacher in the world who would dream that I was doing fast reading when I just stuck my hand in my pocket." Everybody laughed. It seemed like a good joke.

That youth fellowship meeting was about the last one of the school year for our group. I didn't see most of the kids again until the following September. At our first get-together of the fall, one of the kids carne up to me and nearly shouted: "Hey, Ralph, it works!"

"What works?" I asked.

"Braille," he replied. "It's great!"

It seems that that kid, who had been impressed by his blind minister's neat idea, had spent a good part of his summer developing the skills of Braille reading. He had gotten to the point that he could read it far better than I. I have since wondered if our congregation ever heard the fantastic news that its student pastor had been teaching young people how to cheat on exams. I laugh as I think of the situation now.

But, if I laugh at me (and I most certainly do), I spend a lot of time laughing at folks like you, too. Rich experience has taught me that you who are sighted aren't always at your best when you are in the presence of the blind. You are sometimes a bit off pace, and you do the darnedest things.

As an example, let me suppose that I am paying a visit in your home. For the past couple of hours I have been in the living room visiting with hubby and kids. The lady of your house has been in the kitchen whipping up a marvelous concoction of temptations, tastes, and calories. Finally, dinner is ready and the hostess of your home steps into the living room to announce the meal. Almost as an afterthought she says, "Dr. Karstedt, would you like me to show you where the bathroom is?"

I think that it's a fine idea but am too polite to suggest that I sure wish she had asked that question an hour earlier. In my best form I simply say, "Yes, would you please?"

She steers me to the bathroom, projects me through the door, and prepares to shut it after me. Do you know what she does the last thing before latching that door? Sure, you guessed it; she reaches in and flips on the bathroom light. Believe me when I say that that light won't do a thing for me. If it turns you or your spouse on, though, feel free to throw the switch. Pardon me, however, if I take a moment to chuckle.

I'm not kidding about this business. A year or so ago I gave a talk in Logansport, Indiana. In my talk I used this very fictionalized account of my hostess steering me to the bathroom. Everyone in the church roared with delight.

Right after our Sunday afternoon program was over the pastor of the church and his wife invited me to come up to their home for a bit of visiting. When we reached the parsonage, the minister grinned and said, "Let's stop by the bathroom." As I shut the door behind me, I heard an irate wife saying, "George, you didn't turn on the light for him!"

I recall a Saturday evening when I was working very late at my church. It was about 11:00 p.m., and, of course, I had kept the building pitch dark. Why should I waste electricity? In any event I was sitting in my study with the door open to the adjoining hall. I was pondering the next day's sermon and was not making a sound. In short, my study was dark and silent. You get the picture, don't you?

Do you have any idea what happens in a Methodist church at 11:00 p.m. on Saturday? I suspect that it happens in Baptist, Presbyterian, and a myriad of other churches too, but I can't vouch for it. I just know what happens in a Methodist church very late on Saturday night.

Of course, that's the time when at least one Sunday School teacher suddenly remembers that he or she hasn't prepared a lesson and sneaks into the darkened building to retrieve the study book that was left there the previous Sunday. On this Saturday evening it happened just that way. Mrs. S. slipped in through the outside door and stood for a moment in the hall just about five feet from my study door and desk chair. I really wasn't trying to do her in when I turned my head and called, "Hi!" I think, though, that she will never again forget to take her class book home.

Then there was the time when some close friends drove me home from an evening get-together of some sort. My wife, daughter, and dog were not at home at the time (I don't recall now where they were), so I simply said good evening to my friends, shut the outside door behind me, and started up to bed. I went upstairs, undressed, climbed into my pj's , went into the bathroom, washed my face, and started to brush my teeth. Please understand that I am not trying to convince you that I know how to keep myself clean. I am telling this story in rather great detail because I want you to realize that a good deal of time had elapsed. Anyhow, I was in the midst of brushing my teeth when the doorbell rang.

If you have ever lived in a parsonage, you know that a late night phone call or door bell ringing cannot be taken lightly. Usually it declares an emergency situation, and a pastor, hearing it, almost reflexively asks, "Who died?"

When the door bell chimed that evening, I moved quickly. I didn't even take time to spit out my mouth full of toothpaste. I simply dashed downstairs, ran across the living room, flipped the lock on the front door, and pulled the door open. Mumbling a bit through my toothpaste-filled mouth I asked, "Can I help you?"

There were my friends on the porch. "Ralph, are you all right? We didn't see a light and we were worried. It's been over fifteen minutes."

What can I say? Am I supposed to waste electricity in order to make my friends feel good?

I frequently give public talks about my blindness and often allow the listeners to laugh with me in much the same way that I have used these pages to open the door of humor to you. Quite often the talk releases all sorts of feelings and memories within my listeners.

It's been about five years now since a very lovely lady came up to me after such a presentation and thanked me for it. "You helped me get rid of a lot of guilt," she said.

I confess that I was glad to hear that the lady had enjoyed my talk. I must tell you, though, that I was more than a little mystified, because disposing of whatever sort of guilt she had was the furthest thing from my mind. I responded to her words with a questioning, "Oh?"

She went on quickly to tell her tale. "When I was a little girl, grandpa lived with us, and gramps was blind. Mom used to run a string from the back door of our home all the way out to our outhouse. Gramps would simply follow the string, and he got along fine. Well, he got along okay unless some of us kids decided to play a few games. We loved to run that string into the brambles instead of to the privy. We'd slip away a little bit and then watch for grandpa. He'd always go stomping back into the house yelling, 'Sally, those durned kids have done it again!' After I heard your laughter this evening," the woman said, "I got to thinking that maybe gramps didn't mind our tricks so much as I had thought he did. Maybe he laughed a little bit too."

There are times when humor sneaks along behind you and isn't even seen or appreciated until well after the fact. At such times life seems terribly serious. Take, as an example, the story I am about to tell. Fifteen years passed between the time when this frustrating experience took place and the day when I had nerve enough to tell a single soul about it. When my listener began to laugh, I couldn't believe my ears. It took me several more tellings before I found the humor and began to laugh myself.

It was spring of the year 1953 — the end of my senior year at

Shortridge High School in Indianapolis. My sight had taken its final leap into oblivion less than two months earlier, and I was still struggling to come to terms with myself. On one of the last days of school our senior class was to have a picnic at Riverside, a nearby city park, in Indianapolis. When I left for school early that morning, I had already made up my mind that I would not take part in that picnic.

I suppose you would say that I had donned my martyr costume for the day. I didn't want to be a wet blanket on the party. I didn't want to impose on others. I didn't want to put myself in a difficult position. I left for classes filled with the notion that I would spend the day feeling sorry for poor little Ralphie. During the early part of the day I was very successful in fulfilling my intentions.

At last lunchtime came, and I found myself in the school cafeteria chewing on a cheeseburger, and lamenting the plight of poor me. As I sat there mournfully chewing on my not-too-tasty sandwich, I felt a hand placed lightly upon my shoulder. A soft feminine voice said, "Say, would you like to go to the picnic?"

Let me be totally honest; this is no time for dissembling. As best as I can put it into written language, what I heard the voice saying was, "Say, would yo'll lak ta go ta the picnic?"

I stuttered out a questioning "Yes."

The young lady beside my chair said, "I don't drive, but my brothers do. You and I could go on the bus and they'd give you a ride home afterwards."

I gulped out a grateful, "Thank you. It's awfully nice of you."

I heard the voice turning away from me. "I'll pick you up at your locker after school."

The girl must have known where my locker was, because she and her soft accented voice were there waiting for me at the end of the last class period. We started walking down the hall and out of the building towards the bus stop. All at once, I became acutely aware of her accent and of the fact that I didn't know her from Adam, or should I say from Eve?

Do I need to tell you that in the early 1950's Shortridge High School was about 20 percent black, or, as we called it then, Negro? As we climbed on the bus and began to ride, I found that my anxiety level was commencing to soar. She kept "a talkin'", trying to fill my silence with her conversation. I just sat and fretted and fumed. Who was I out with anyhow? Was I having what amounted almost to a date with a Negro? The more she talked, the more I fretted. The situation became nearly intolerable.

We reached the park, and my heavily-accented girl friend and I got off the bus and began to walk towards the picnic area. I finally reached the point that I could contain myself no longer.

"Pardon me for asking;" I said, "this is a terrible question, and I don't know how to ask it, but . . . Well, you know that I don't know you, and . . . Well, I'm sure you realize that you have an accent, and . . . Well, I can't see you, and I need to know. . . Are you from the south, or are you Ne . . . Ne . . . Negro?"

I want to kick myself every time I remember asking that terrible question. I am squirming inside myself as I sit and type out these words. I'm really not sure that I should tell you the answer that she gave me, but I suspect that you won't read another word if I don't.

She was from the south. She was a nice little white girl who had just moved up from Atlanta. I was "safe."

But what difference did it make? I realize now that at that moment I was truly blind. I was so worried about a skin color that I couldn't see anyhow, that I was unable to recognize a truly beautiful young woman who had seen a scared and troubled kid and had said, "Can I help you?" The color of that girl's skin should have been totally incidental. Had she been purple and green with orange polka dots, she would still have been a beautiful person. I kick myself again and again as I recall that incident, and pray that God will free me from ever being so blind again.

Do you see why I have had a hard time laughing about that particular incident? Audiences to whom I tell it find themselves chuckling before I have really commenced the tale. Perhaps you have found yourself smiling as you have read. There is humor in it — great humor. After all, what is humor but tragedy drawn to its extreme? To put the matter another way: you have to laugh when it hurts too much to cry.

Let me tell you one more story that sits upon that poorly defined boundary between hilarity and tragedy. It happened during my first day in classes at Butler University. To be specific, it took place in the 9:00 a.m. freshman English class.

Dr. Hornback, our English prof, decided to start all of his freshman students off by asking us to write an impromptu in-class theme. He told us that we had the entire 50-minute period to get the work done. As the class made energetic noises with pencil and pen, I stepped up to the teacher's desk and asked him how he wanted to handle the situation. "I don't carry my typewriter with me," I explained in a whisper.

"That's all right, Karstedt," Dr. Hornback replied. "You can do the work at home this evening. Use your typewriter; give yourself 50 minutes; write your paper; and bring it in to me tomorrow. It won't be any problem at all."

I did it. I went home and immediately went to my room and placed paper in machine. I checked my Braille watch for the correct time. (Of course I didn't turn on the lights; why waste electricity?) Then I began to type.

At the end of the allotted time my paper was done. I happily took its sheets, folded them into neat thirds, and placed them in an envelope. I was so honest that I even sealed the envelope.

That evening my parents asked if they could look at my paper. "Not on your life," I replied. "Those other guys in class didn't have their folks looking over their themes. You don't get to either." I marvel at myself as I write these words. I can't bring myself to believe how scrupulous I was back then.

The impression that I am trying to leave with you is that when I took my paper in to class it was totally unseen by any human eye. That is absolutely true.

When I went into class, I handed Dr. Hornback my sealed envelope and waited anxiously for his comments. I remember hearing him tear the envelope open, and I recall the ruffle of paper as he leafed through my carefully typed sheets. At last he spoke to the class and to me: "I want you to know," he said, "that Karstedt here is the only one who has turned in a paper without a single mistake on it."

Wow! Wasn't that great? A blind kid had turned in the only paper without a single blunder. I had a hard time believing that my typing had been that good.

Then my professor cleared his throat and told the rest of the story. "Karstedt, you must have had that machine of yours set on stencil (white). There isn't a single readable word on this paper."

At the risk of repeating myself, may I ask if you begin to understand: "You have to laugh when it hurts too much to cry."

"Maybe," says the parent as she gives an indulgent smile. "Maybe."
The hopeful child dances with expectation:
   "Perhaps I can."
   "She says that it may be possible."
   "I think that it's going to be okay."
Yet the parent's intent was not so positive:
   "I couldn't stand to say no."
   "Of course he can't."
   "Surely I have begun to soften the disappointment."
And thus the simple "maybe" has become the agency both of hope
   and of frustration,
For its quiet promise has intensified the pain of the intended denial.

A Door Ajar

Any blind person can tell you about the dangers that are directed towards him because of a door that has been left half open. I experienced the pain of it yesterday evening as I started through our kitchen on my way to give my poodle his night outing. Someone had opened a kitchen cabinet in order to get a tool and had left the cabinet door standing straight out. I wonder if you get the point as vividly as my forehead did? Had the door been left shut, or had it been opened fully to the hundred and eighty degree point, I would have passed in total safety. Partially open as it was, the door was a nearly unavoidable enemy for me as I started my hurried journey through the kitchen.

The story is almost always the same. Leave a door open and a blind man will pass through it. Leave it shut, and he will quickly discover the fact that it is closed. Leave it half open, and he is very likely to bump his head or crack his shin.

Let me be clear in saying that I am not accusing my family of intentionally ambushing me with that cabinet door. I know that they left that door swung half open either in thoughtless haste or in the incorrect belief that I would not be passing through that area before they would have returned the tool and closed the cabinet once more. It is with this figure of speech that I want to begin a very important discussion. A door ajar is far more than a cabinet in Ralph's kitchen. It is a symbolic reference to the pain-evoking barriers that are thoughtlessly and unintentionally placed in the pathways of many blind and otherwise handicapped people.

Let me give you some examples of what I mean. During the year 1979 a specially-formed task force of my United Methodist Church was hard at work surveying and analyzing the unique problems that come to handicapped people in our society and particularly in the life of our denomination's ministries. The task force went out of its way to open as many doors as it possibly could to handicapped men and women. In short, it was on the side of the handicapped. If all of its recommendations were taken seriously, almost every United Methodist congregation would immediately undertake major projects building wheelchair ramps, widening rest room doors, putting Church School literature in Braille and on recordings, and doing a host of other things that are intended to open our church to the handicapped.

Because I am a blind person who happens to be a United Methodist pastor, I was put on the task force's mailing list and was allowed to read the minutes, copies of the correspondence, and the conclusions that came to and rose out of the committee. Practically every bit of writing to and from the task force spoke in behalf of the handicapped and came from "friends." As I read, I was sometimes reminded of the old saying: "With friends like these, who needs enemies?"

A lady, expert in the matters of handicap, wrote to the task force saying that "the blind and epileptic can not become ministers, if for no other reason than the fact that they can not drive a car." As a blind minister I was thunderstruck by her words. She was telling me, and the rest of society too, that I could not be something that I already was. It was this lady's thoughtless and well-intentioned remark that gave birth to my doctoral study on the subject of *The Impact Of My Physical Blindness Upon My Ministry At The Burlington United Methodist Church*. No matter what this lady said, I knew that I could be a minister. I decided to start a study that would evaluate the effects of my blindness and to show why they were not prohibitive to pastoral success.

But let me make the point as clearly as I am able. This witness to our United Methodist task force was speaking in behalf of the blind. She was, however, trying to be fair. In her attempt to be realistic she sold me, and any other blind person who might aspire to the Christian ministry, right down the drain.

Let me tell you about the first time that I ran into this sort of attitude. It happened in April of my senior year in high school. I have already told you that my sight finally left me in one climactic gush that had come to me in March of that year. Well, I had stayed at home and away from classes for some two or three weeks at the time when I entered total blindness. In early April I returned to school and commenced my last few weeks before graduation.

I shall never forget the first full day in classes. The provocation came to me at the end of my fourth period English class. As the class responded to the closing buzzer and headed towards the door, the teacher called me to the front of the room. She took me off into a corner and said something like this: "Ralph, I like you very much. You are a very nice boy. I would hate to see you hurt yourself. You know that you are no longer going to be able to do the things that you used to do. I don't want to see you trying anything too hard. Like I said, I don't want you to hurt yourself."

To this day I do not know for sure what that English teacher meant. I do know what a scared kid heard her saying. In effect, I heard her telling me to sit on my bottom until the day I died. After all, I was blind. I shouldn't be expected to do anything of importance.

Perhaps my understanding of her words was enforced by memories of trips that I had taken down East Washington Street in Indianapolis. I remember many childhood trips down that street, as I walked with my mother on her way to the bank. In each of the walks we had passed two, three, or more blind beggars with pencils, accordions, violins, and tin cups. Armed by such memories, I was torn apart by the teacher's words. As I heard them I found my spine going rigid. I was really frightened.

A moment ago I wrote that I did not know the teacher's intentions. As I think back now I try to give her the benefit of the doubt. Perhaps she was simply telling me to be cautious. I suspect that she had absolutely no conception of the weight her words were to carry as they fell upon me. I know that there must have been a sense in which she was simply reflecting concern. The fact remains, however, that she gave me a verbal blow that could have initiated the process of social paralysis within me.

Let me offer another example. This one comes from relatively recent history.

In April, 1980, my United Methodist Church held its General Conference at the Indianapolis Convention Center. As an Indiana pastor who was involved with the task force related to persons with handicapping conditions, I was invited to meet with a group who wished to assure the accessibility of that conference to the handicapped. After all, the General Conference of our denomination meets only once every four years. It is by far the most important meeting in the regular life of the church.

Our committee met one snowy day in late February. We discussed everything that we could think of. We talked about wheelchair access, rest room availability, floor level seating that would not require the handicapped to climb stairs, and signing of all sessions for the benefit of the deaf. By the time we were finished, we believed that we had done everything we could to guarantee full participation by handicapped people.

On the second day of the General Conference we were shown how wrong we could be. Our embarrassment came when Dr. Howard Rice, stated clerk of the Presbyterian Church, approached the speakers' platform to bring fraternal greetings from his denomination. The crippled clergyman rolled up to the steps of the platform in his wheelchair. You guessed it; there was no ramp!

Our capable ushers covered up the situation the best that they could. Four of them were swift in surrounding the wheelchair and lifting our guest to the elevated area of the lectern. Do I need to tell you that by the time of the next morning's session a ramp to the rostrum had been erected?

I guess there are twin lessons that can be learned from this experience. The first is that the Church, and our society with it, is not prepared to think of the handicapped as its leaders. We speak energetically about the things that we can do for those people, but we have not brought ourselves to the realization that they can do a great deal for us. Although we do not intend to do so, we institute, or at least fail to relieve, the pressures that keep them from assuming leadership among us.

I said that there were two lessons. The second one is that anyone of us can get caught in the tender trap. I was myself in the committee that did not plan for a wheelchair ramp to the platform. I know how easy it is to simply overlook the contributions that handicapped people can offer society. For this reason alone, I do not intend to write with accusing fingers. Rather I speak out of intensified understanding.

What we are discussing is a door left ajar. It is the frustration inherent in the word "maybe." It is society saying "yes, we want to give you a chance, but . . ." But blind people who can't drive cars surely can't be ministers . . . But people with severe handicaps can't be expected to carry the same load that others do . . . But of course there won't be anyone in a wheel chair who will need to go to the lectern. Remember, when a blind man bumps into a door left ajar, he can be hurt very badly.

Let me tell one more personal account. My father went into retirement and onto Social Security while I was yet in college. Because

I was at that time the handicapped dependent of a Social Security recipient, I too was given a monthly check. I accepted it while I was in school. Everyone told me that I should.

Following seminary I assumed the ministry of a full-time church and began to receive a full-time salary. Knowing the laws of the land, I went with dad to the Social Security office with the word that I no longer needed or deserved my monthly payment. I cannot describe the reluctance of the Social Security worker to take my name off the lists. I was blind. I was handicapped. I did not need to earn my own living. "Please son, feel free to apply for your checks again whenever you decide that you can't earn a full-time salary."

Through words and a number of personal illustrations I have been attempting to describe a phenomenon that is sometimes called *The Making Of Blind Men*. The title comes from a superb book that was written by Robert A. Scott a number of years back. In the book Scott insists that we as a society take sightless persons and turn them into "blind men" through the various words and unspoken concepts that we teach.

The schools for the blind that are sponsored by most of our states offer an excellent case in point. The schools have been established at a huge expense to the taxpayer and out of the very best of motives. We want to take care of our blind children.

But how do we do it? We put them together as a group on their own campuses and teach them how to live successfully among other blind persons. When the sightless children go home on summer vacations, they tend to feel like strangers in a foreign land. When they graduate they are inclined to seek the company of other blind persons. More often than not, they end up spending their employed years working in a sheltered workhouse for the blind. After all, the very isolation that has been imposed upon them because of their special schooling has prepared them to be different than other people. It has taught them that security can only be found when they are among "their own."

I am convinced that these words reflect far more than theory. During the last few years I have been chairman of a special Annual Conference church group whose purpose is that of recruiting blind persons for our North Indiana (United Methodist) Conference's various camps. We have worked hard to attract blind students to our regular camps, and we have attempted to include them within our regular events. We want the blind children to associate with the sighted, so that they can get the feeling of what it is to live and to be accepted in the full scope of society.

I must frankly tell you that we have had only very slight success in our recruitment efforts. The sightless children who have come to our camps have enjoyed them completely. For the most part they have wanted to return. Most of Indiana's blind children, however, prefer a camp for blind children only that is offered by another denomination. They are far more comfortable with their friends than in a world of strangers. Is it hard to extend the pattern to know that these same young people will spend most of their lives in sheltered workhouses and living among their other sightless friends? The pattern for them has already been set. It will be extremely hard for any of them to emerge from the protective cocoon of isolation and to walk and work in the world of ordinary society.

Parents fall into the trap as easily as does anyone else. They say: "He's blind. We can't expect him to . . ."

A few years ago a young man, whom I shall call George, was brought to my home to spend the weekend. George was about 20 and was trying to figure out the course for his life. His minister thought that I, as another blind person, might be able to assist him in his choices.

As I talked to George, I discovered that his mother had made a habit of removing him from everything. She took him out of the school for the blind when she saw that dorm life was sometimes rough and tumble. She took him out of regular high school when she felt that the teachers did not have enough sympathy. She withdrew him from college because classes were too hard. She personally gave him all of the help that she could muster, and she protected him from everything.

George had been driven to our house early on Saturday afternoon. We spent the afternoon and evening getting acquainted. Then it came time for sleep and I steered him up to his bedroom.

As George undressed he handed me his pants saying, "Hang these up, will you?"

I took them and started to do it. All at once I stopped and said, "Why? Why don't you hang them up?"

"I can't," George replied. "I'm blind."

I reached out and pushed the pants back into George's hands. "Welcome to the club!" I said. "Hang up your own pants." I don't know how straight he got them on the hanger, but he most assuredly did hang them up.

To be sure, blind people do have limitations. For that matter we all do. For the most part, though, the magnitude of these limitations is exaggerated and, through the exaggeration, is reinforced.

I openly admit that as a blind man I cannot drive an auto. I admit that it would be most foolish for me to attempt judging an art festival. I admit that it would be hard for me to adjudicate at a Miss America pageant — unless, of course, Braille would be acceptable. Don't tell me, though, that I can't preach a sermon, or lead a bike camp, or play the violin. I have a host of friends and parishioners who could be quick to tell you that you are very wrong.

Even the best and the most open-minded and accepting of us, however, continue to say it. We say, "Of course the blind — the handicapped — deserve a chance. They can do lots of things, but . . ."

I myself, have never known the full force of society's thoughtless thrust to turn sightless persons into "blind men." I suppose that there are a number of reasons.

For one, I was nearly out of public school before I lost my sight. Thus I was free from all of the subtle pressures that are imposed by schools and agencies for the blind.

Again, my parents were not the sort of people who could easily settle for less than the possible. Mom had never spoken to me about whether or not I should go to college. It had always been simply assumed that I would do so. After all, a college background was, in her way of thinking, germinal to educated success. Even when I lost my sight, it did not occur to my folks or to me that I would do anything but go ahead as planned. I shall be eternally grateful for the motivation and understanding that my folks gave me.

Again, I was not weighed down by financial needs. I was extremely fortunate that my parents had enough available money to see me through the college and seminary years. Had the financial situation been different, I would doubtless have found my position infinitely more difficult.

I must also confess that I have been blessed with an adequate brain. The fact that I have been able to earn four college and graduate degrees, most of them with honors, attests to this. I do not write of these things boastfully. I am, indeed, very grateful.

I did, you see, have a number of things going for me. I keep thinking of the many sightless persons who have been chained to their world of the blind and whose abilities could have given them freedom if they only had had the chance. A sightless person is very fortunate if he is not turned into a "blind man."

I suppose that the heaviest chains that I have worn because of my sightlessness have been those of what I call "downgrading." I recall visiting with a district superintendent shortly before I came into the North Indiana Conference of my church. I asked this leader of the church what sort of problems I would have because of my blind state. After thinking a minute, he told me that I would probably always be placed in a church about one level less than what my abilities would otherwise indicate.

The average person may not think of it, or even want to think of it in this way, but within the ecclesiastical structure churches are often rated. There are different qualities of pastoral appointments. Qualities are poorly defined but clearly recognized. They relate to church size, pastoral salary, missional influence, average attendance, quality of church building and parsonage, etc. Well, I was told that I would always be one level beneath that of my abilities.

When I first heard that statement, I accepted it. After all, I thought that my blindness surely would limit my pastoral performance in some definite way. As the years have passed I have become convinced that I was absolutely wrong! I believe that I can substantiate the opinion that my blindness has in many ways been a source of strength for my ministry, and that I am at least as effective as I might have been had I not lost my sight.

The foregoing statement may seem a bit strange and strained. In a later chapter I will attempt to explain and document it. At the moment, simply accept my conviction that it is so.

The fact is that, although my pastoral record is solid, and even though my recent doctoral study clearly shows the power that my blindness can bring to ministry, I continue to be assigned to pastoral appointments that are in salary and size less than those of other pastors with comparable experience and education. My own church, which has every right to know me well, continues to say to me, "Yes, but . . ."

Permit another story. I love to travel. I especially enjoy attending conferences and conventions. I have also learned to expect certain things as I wander.

It is nearly inevitable that at a convention I will be approached by several different people who will ask me if I am Brown from Wisconsin, Jones from Michigan, or Smith from Florida. It is my custom to smile and simply say that I am Karstedt from Indiana. I always go on to ask a question of my own. "What made you think that I was Brown, Jones, or Smith?"

I am sure that you know the answer. The person who has approached me will stutter a bit and then say, "Well, he's blind too."

I have some personal ideas about the people in question. I picture Brown as being tall, while I am only five foot seven. I imagine Jones with a bushy head of hair, while I am going bald. I see Smith as one who is fat as a tub, whereas my personal paunch isn't quite that large yet. I suspect that Brown, Jones, and Smith all get very tired of being asked if they are Karstedt from Indiana.

I don't really mind being blind. As these pages will illustrate, I certainly don't mind writing and talking about it. I become positively livid, however, when folks spend so much time looking at my eyes that they can't see me.

My name is Ralph. I love to read murder mysteries, to ride a tandem bike with my wife, and to teach speech. I have my own peculiar sets of loves, hurts, and hangups. In short, I am not like any other person in this world. Like *every* other man or woman I am unique. When, I wonder, will people stop looking at my non-functioning eyes and be able to see me for who I am?

A moment ago I was talking about my church and its regard of me as a minister. I told you that about three years ago it asked me to chair the task force on the inclusion of blind persons in our summer camps. I was later asked to lead the section of our camps and conferences program that relates to our camping enterprises on behalf of all "special" persons. I am really very proud of these camps. Because of them our conference gave camping opportunities to 179 retarded young people and adults and 160 deaf people during the last summer alone. I am glad to have the opportunity to work within these camps and will do all I can for them.

But why does my church see me only in regard to my handicap? Why can't it recognize me as a preacher? Why did it wait for twenty years before asking me to serve on any of its other boards and agencies? It would seem that the temptation is almost irresistible for a blind person to be recognized because of his non-functioning eyes, rather than his totality of potentials and possibilities. I have concluded that I may as well stop grumbling and take advantage of the situations that come to me.

In a sense I suppose that this book can be seen as an example of my willingness to live within my orb of blindness. A few years ago I could never have brought myself to write it. In those years I insisted that I was a minister who just happened to be blind. "I am not a blind minister." Perhaps I have surrendered a bit of myself as I have commenced these pages. I prefer to believe that I have come to a partial settlement with a social reality that offers me pastoral possibility. Is this double talk? I hope not.

My position within the structure of our special camps has already given me a number of unique insights. Two years ago, for instance, I had a telephone call from Mrs. H. who is the mother of two girls in their early twenties. As the mother explained the story to me, her daughters, Susan and Sally, were both blind and somewhat retarded. She said that the girls loved music and she wondered if they could fit into our camp for musicians which is known as Epworth Forest Choir School. I gave the matter long thought, consulted with the executive director of Choir School, and concluded that retardation was the real problem which the girls faced. Neither the director nor I could imagine that Susan or Sally could possibly learn the Bach, Handel, and other quite sophisticated music that Choir School regularly performs. I realized that I, myself, have a hard enough time with it. I could not conceive of retarded persons even beginning to tangle with it.

I talked again with the mother and suggested that her daughters might enjoy taking part in one of our camps for retarded persons. She was enthusiastic in her agreement. It was then that the fun began.

It seemed that the leadership team of our retarded camping program was afraid of having a blind person, much less two of them, in camp. All sorts of reasons were given to explain why they should not be accepted for the camp. The girls' minister and I found a response to each of them. No matter how hard we worked and talked, however, the bottom line answer remained "No!" Susan and Sally had their applications for our camps for the retarded returned to them. They had been denied acceptance.

As I write these pages, I can now tell a tale that has a very happy ending. Following a winter that was punctuated with letters and phone calls from me, Mrs. H., and the girls' pastor, the retarded camp's leadership team agreed to give Susan and Sally a try. Rather stringent requirements were set for the trial effort, because the girls' home church had to agree to supply, at its own cost, one adult helper who could accompany Susan and another to be with Sally for the week. In effect there was a compromise which allowed the girls to have their

chance and which assured camp personnel that no undue and unrealistic burdens would be placed upon them.

During Susan and Sally's week at camp, I had no news of them
at all. I was, during those same days, out on the bike leading junior
highs along the back roads of northern Indiana. I got back from bike
camp late on Friday and heard the word about the H. girls the following afternoon. My Saturday nap was interrupted by a phone call from
Mrs. H., who wanted to thank me for helping her girls have "the best
week in their lives." That afternoon marked one of the best moments
in my life. I smile now as I hear various members of the retarded camp's
staff talk of the way they took blind girls into their program last year
and of how the girls did so well that they have already been invited
back.

Susan and Sally's story is that of a door that was finally thrown
wide open. Think back, though, to the time a year earlier when no
such opening seemed possible. Can you imagine the frustration that
must have filled those young ladies and their parents? They certainly
knew the terrible pain of a "Yes, but . . ." answer and the hurt that
can be imposed by a door that has been left ajar.

In order to keep records absolutely straight, I must say that I feel
it very proper for responsible people to ask sensible questions about
the handicapped. I recall a pastor-parish committee (many denomi-
nations would use the term pulpit committee for this group) which
once interviewed me. They asked me many questions as to how I,
as a blind person, would be able to do the various tasks that would
be mine as their minister. I had two reactions in regard to that meeting with the committee.

My first reaction was that I would have asked the same questions
had our situations been reversed. I think that any responsible committee member would want to make sure that the pastor chosen for
his or her church would be able to attend to the tasks that would be
his. To my mind the committee asked reasonable and normal questions. When the questioning was over their attitude was very open-
minded and accepting. In this regard I certainly appreciated their acceptance of responsibility.

My second reaction is that the committee was so busy asking questions about my blindness that its members did not once question my
theology, concepts of churchmanship, and specific beliefs in ministry. These should have been the first and foremost questions that they
asked. Like others before and after them the committee members were

so concerned about my lack of sight that they were unable to recognize the really crucial and relevant issues. In effect, my blindness had served as a smoke screen.

I have written about attitudes that have been spelled out by the words "maybe," "yes, but . . .," and "a door ajar." These attitudes are far more subtle than were the simple "no's" that were thrown at handicapped persons in earlier years and centuries. Because they are more subtle, however, they are far harder to deal with.

Remember, a blind man can cope with a door that is shut or one that is wide open. I guess that he can deal with one that has been left ajar too. He can, that is, if he isn't hurt too badly by the bump.

I don't want to suffer, Lord;
I have no appetite for pain;
I have absolutely no desire to experience the mortification of my flesh.
I don't want to suffer; please take this cup from me.
  I would be youthful and healthy all of my life;
  I would dance and sing in a continuing celebration of vitality;
  I would salute the power of who I am.
  Don't speak of suffering; take the cup from me.
I am disturbed by the limitations of my body;
Fading vision, thinning hair, lessened potency, and aching bones all
      frighten me;
I must forever retain the power of my youthful years.
I am bothered by my aging body; take this cup from me.
  But now I must confess a glimmer of new understanding,
  For I know that a river is given its force by the banks that hold it in,
  And a picture without shadows suffers from the lack of richness,
  I ponder such insights with uncertainty, for the cup of my
      finiteness seems yet an enemy.
I struggle with thoughts that transcend my bones,
And think of one who was crucified;
I sense that there is a strength that is induced by pain,
But I can not desire it, for it is a bitter cup.
  And now I hold that cup in trembling hands;
  I do not want it, but I can not turn it down;
  Instinctively I know that, if it drops and shatters, I too will be spilled
      forever,
  And now I drink and discover the unexpected taste of life.

You Can't Keep A Good Man Down

A tale has been told concerning a pair of missionaries who were captured by cannibals. The first of the missionaries had been cooked and consumed by the hungry natives, and the second was in the pot waiting for the fire to be lit beneath him. At this moment the collection of cannibals became ill, and all of the natives began retching and vomiting. Surveying the group from his position in the pot, the second man of God observed, "Boys, I told you that you couldn't keep a good man down."

There may be those who will say that this story is in poor taste. In so far as I am concerned it makes a very powerful point. Within my personal world of experience and of faith there is the conviction that somehow, somewhere, someone is willing and able to help the children of men to meet the challenges of their lives. I express this thought carefully and yet clearly, for to me it has become an article of faith.

Folks have often asked me what it was like for me to lose my sight. I reply quite honestly and tell them that it was scary as all get out.

I was approaching my eighteenth birthday when my vision left me completely. During the previous couple of years I had experienced a series of retinal hemorrhages, each of which threw a heavy cloud over such sight as I had and left me with a bit less vision than I had possessed before. I think objectively as I write these words today. Back in the time of my teens, when all of these sight-siphoning events were taking place, I was just plain scared.

It is a scary business to climb out of bed in the morning and to be unsure if it will be safe for you to enter into the events of the day. "Will my eyes be good enough to let me cross the street?" "Can I go into that strange place without getting lost?" "Can I attend that party without making a complete fool of myself?" Questions such as these torment the mind and draw restrictive bands about the spirit.

It is very frightening to continually face the fact that some day you will be blind. I remember a bus ride that found me going downtown at the end of a school day way back during my junior year at Short-ridge High. A blind man, white cane in hand, climbed onto the bus just a stop or two after I had boarded. He sat down right in front of me. I observed that man as he rode along and listened for the driver to call out his getting-off place. I watched as he stepped down from the bus and, cane swinging before him, moved out into the chaotic swarm of downtown humanity. My body became increasingly tense as I saw him moving away, and I found myself thinking, "My God, I would rather die than have to face up to that!"

But I did have to face up to it. Even as I rode that after-school bus, I knew in my inner self that blindness would some day be my lot. I lived constantly with the uncertainty of my abilities to handle the events of today and with the certainty that tomorrow would find me walking in a world of darkness. It was, as I have already said, a very scary business.

I am now able to look back upon the frightening days that I have been describing and to see something that was not very obvious to me then. In retrospect I am able to recognize a quality of faith that was even more profound than the fright of which I have been telling you. My faith was unthought and unarticulated, for it lay in the gut level of my life. Exactly because it rested in this core of who I was, my faith was strong enough to see me through.

I was going to "make it." I realize now that I never once seriously doubted that fact. I was going to make it. I was going to be "success-ful!" Although I was sometimes scared half stiff as I walked through my fading world, I never really questioned my ability to make it and be successful. I never once sat back and pondered the question of whether or not I would be able to have a decent sort of life. I simply took it for granted that somehow, some way, I would find "success."

Please note that I have placed the word "success" in quotation marks. I have done this intentionally because I know that the word means different things to different persons. To some people "success," or being "successful," means playing third base for the New York Yankees. To some it means being a millionaire. A lovely wife, five healthy kids, and a home in the country spell out "success" for some folks. Winning the Miss America pageant fulfills the word's definition for others.

Let me tell you what I have always meant by "success." To me the term means being able to earn your own way in life, being able to provide for a family and a home, being a productive person who can leave a contribution in life, and being the sort of person who can leave this world knowing that he or she has given a bit more than he has taken. That's what I mean by "success," and within the bounds of that definition I never once questioned my ability to have it.

Let me hasten to tell you that back then I didn't think, talk, and sound like a preacher. I hang my head a bit as I write that I had not attended church as often as I might have, and that I had not read the Bible as much as I should have. I did not have churchy language at my command. I could not think and speak with the sophisticated words of "theologese." I had a simple gut-level trust that communicated with my emotional self and conveyed the wordless message that somehow, somewhere, someone was on my side, and I was going to "make it."

Years have passed and I now have the background of theology, of Scripture, and of experience within the Church that can enable me to use all of the right words. I can now speak learnedly about omnipotence and about grace. I can, for instance, quote from the Psalms and declare that we must "Know that the Lord is God! It is He that made us, and we are His." Again I can remind you that "the Lord is good; His steadfast love endures for ever, and His faithfulness to all generations." (Psalm 100)

In short the verbalized faith that I express today says that God is God and that God is good. It is my belief that a good God will always enable His sons and daughters to meet the challenges that come to them in a world that He has fashioned and formed. I believe these words completely. I know, though, that they came to me after the fact. The faith of my inner self, that of my guts, spoke to me long before I was able to speak the theological phrases that I have mentioned.

How then did I gain my perspective of trust? As I reflect on this matter, I look back thankfully to a pair of loving parents. Mom and dad so surrounded me with love and with their own profound faithfulness that I developed a sense of emotional trust from the earliest days of my life. They loved me. They supported me. They believed in me and enveloped me with their own trusting natures. Of course they, themselves, had grown up in Christian homes and their reverence was real. I soaked it up without knowing that I was doing so, and when I needed it most, it was there without my recognizing it. Thank God.

I have a prayer that I offer almost nightly for my daughter and for those who are close to me. It is that she, that they, will be able to soak up the same sort of gut-level faith that has served me so very well. To be a bit more pointed, let me say that my prayer asks God to enable me to share the quality of loving and trusting that can give a sense of security and faithfulness. As I write these words I offer an extra amen.

What place does formal theology then have in our world? It has a very important role to play, and it should never be discounted. Theological study helps us to examine and to understand the deep feelings that are within us. It also enables us to test our emotional inklings so that we may differentiate between those that are solid and true and those which are spurious and may take us off the "deep end" of life. I am in no way calling for theological irresponsibility. I am only insisting that, for me at least, emotion that is generated through life's experience is the very center of faith, and that it is defined, refined, and checked out by the words that men think and speak.

Let me turn a mental corner and deal with another sort of concern. I have often spoken of the inner-self faith that saw me through the days of my entry into blindness. I have usually received very satisfying feedback from congregations and community clubs to which I have spoken with words like these. I have always been a little bothered, though, by the discovery that my words of faithfulness seem to have a greater appeal to the healthy and hearty than they do to those who are currently involved in critical situations of handicap.

Have I been too pious? Have I sounded like a victorious soul who has found all of the answers and who is no longer involved in the struggle of today and tomorrow? Have I presented myself as being so perfect in faith and victory that my words have had the sound of unreality in the ears of those who are up to their necks in current suffering and striving? In short, have I oversimplified and have I suggested that everyone who believes and trusts will have lilies and roses the rest of his days? I have not intended to present such an image. It may be, though, that I have.

It is always easy to look back in hindsight and to speak of the faith that has seen you through. It is infinitely more difficult to recognize the faith that is operative in the circumstances of the critical present.

Let me say very clearly that I continue to encounter the inevitable struggles of life. In recent years, for example, I have experienced a certain amount of high frequency hearing loss. Although I know such a loss to be totally natural for a man in his mid-forties, I must confess to a horrendous shock wave that batters at the walls of my feelings.

Let it be said to any person who is in the continuing struggle of living that our lives are finite and bodily disintegration and death are constantly before us. No quality of faith can remove the spectors of cancer, heart failure, arthritis, impotency, and ultimately the grave from our futures. It is natural for us to feel a bit of scare as we are confronted with these forces. The faith that I have been writing about does not pretend that such frightening factors do not exist; it declares that we can "make it" even in their midst.

Let me tell you the story of Ethel. Ethel and her husband Earl used to live in a country home near Sheridan, Indiana. It was spring of 1965, and I was pastor of a small country church about a mile from their home.

On the evening of Palm Sunday a collection of tornadoes struck Indiana. They raked the state in a pattern that drew lines of destruction from Elkhart County in the north, south to the central state area where I was pastoring. One of the tornadoes came through our community. It removed the corner of our church's roof, destroyed many homes in the area, and took nine lives at the rural crossroads just beyond our church. Ethel's husband Earl was one of those who was killed.

Ethel and Earl had been spending that Palm Sunday evening watching television. When Ethel heard the storm approaching with its freight train-like roar, she threw herself down on the living room floor and screamed for Earl to do the same thing. Unfortunately, Earl's hearing was very poor, and he neither heard the coming storm nor understood his wife's words. When the twister hit with all its demoniac force, it killed Earl instantly, wrapped Ethel up in the living room rug, and threw her carpet-protected body out into the family's east yard. Hours passed before Ethel's grandson came on the scene and discovered his imprisoned and frightened grandma.

I visited Ethel in the Noblesville hospital on the morning after all of this tragic action took place. I was a badly shaken young pastor who was facing the prospect of multiple funerals and who didn't have any appropriate words for a hurting and lonely widow. I had worries that were totally groundless. When I entered Ethel's room, that dear lady began to sympathize with me because of the very hard job I had before me. I had never seen anything like it in all my life.

May I speak of Janice. She had an unbelievable world of medical problems. Janice's youngest son had been born with multiple birth defects. At the most recent count, he had undergone better than fifty operations that had caused hospitalizations to be the punctuation point in the account of his life's first dozen years. Janice, herself, was a very severe diabetic who was suffering kidney failure and a number of other serious ailments.

During the early years of my ministry at the church Janice and her family brought their membership into our congregation. She spoke frequently of her faith. From time to time people would question Janice about her trust and ask her how she could possibly believe in God with all of the problems that she had heaped upon her. With Job-like faithfulness she always responded by saying, "I couldn't put up with all these problems if I didn't believe in God." Janice died a few years ago. I found it symbolic that her passing was on Easter Sunday. Her defeat and victory over death were portrayed in the occurrence.

Ethel and Janice are both witnesses to the sort of faith that moves with quiet intensity within the darkened and frightening experiences of life. They knew how terrible life's forces can sometimes be. They also carried within them the inner faithfulness that made it totally impossible for anything to really get them down. Theirs is the sort of faith that I have been writing about.

I have told you about the way I lost my sight in a climactic burst of hemorrhaging during March of my senior high school year. May I now share a bit more of the story.

Following my vision loss I had many adjustments to make. By the grace of God and that of Joel Hadley, our high school principal, I did manage to graduate that spring from my Indianapolis high school. Immediately after graduation, I enrolled in a touch-typing course at the Lane Business College in the city.

That summer of 1953 I spent three evenings a week at the business college and finally managed to work my typing up to a more or less respectable twenty-five words a minute. As I think retrospectively about that summer I wonder how I was able to do it. My brother had taken an air force leave to come home in early June for my graduation. While home he had purchased a new (for him) two-year-old Ford. Along with two other young men he started driving to California where he was to report for duty at the Castle Air Force Base near

Merced. Dale never made it. On the afternoon of my June 19th birthday we got a telegram reporting his death in an early morning Kansas head-on collision.

Where did I get the time to study all of that typing? How did mom and dad maintain enough energy to haul me uptown every Monday, Wednesday, and Friday evening so that I could take my classes? How did any of us manage to cast any sort of positive gaze towards the future? I look back and shake my head in wonder. The fact is, though, that I did it; we did it. Something inside all of us said that I, that we, would "make it."

In early August I completed my crash course in touch typing and sent an enrollment application in to Butler University, a fine college on the north side of our city. A week or so later I got an acceptance statement from Butler. The day after I received my official acceptance, I opened my mail and discovered a rush letter from a university fraternity. The letter invited me to attend a fraternity party that was to be held during the evening of one of the school's opening days. It suggested that I might be a candidate for fraternity membership. I was delighted! I was so pleased that I replied to the invitation by telephone rather than by the much slower mail. "Thank you for inviting me. I'll be glad to come."

As I started out for the fraternity house that Monday afternoon I was filled with nice thoughts about the generous college guys who were willing to think of a blind kid as a future frat brother. When I reached the house, I discovered the truth. Those fraternity fellows didn't know that I was blind. They had checked the university's enrollment list and had discovered that I was male, that I was white, and that I was to enter Butler that fall. I must have struck them with the force of a wet mop as I walked into their house that afternoon.

Let me be totally fair. The guys showed me a good time. They helped me roast my hot dogs and sat around and visited politely for a couple of hours. Then they offered to drive me home.

It was during the drive home that the fellows told me the facts of life. It seemed that they had to have at least a "C" average if their house was to be able to hold dances and to participate in intramural activities. They were already on the verge of sinking below the requisite "C." They said, "We like you, Karstedt, but . . . Well, we figure that you're going to flunk out, and we don't dare let you drag us down." That's the way it was.

May I tell you that I was a scared kid as I entered upon my

college career? The fraternity men had topped off my already heaped bucket of fears and uncertainties. If you have ever seen a scared little dog running down the road with his tail between his legs, you have seen a pretty fair likeness of me at the time I entered college. I didn't know how to be more scared than I was. I was so frightened that I started working.

Although my public school academic record had never been bad, it had never been very hot either. I hadn't really learned how to work hard in my studies. It all changed during that fall of '53. Ralph started working harder than he knew how to work, and then the results began to come in.

I finished the first semester of my freshman year with a grade point average of 3.59 (4.0 would have been straight-A.) By then I knew the trick, and I had begun to develop both a measure of self-confidence and a reputation to preserve. To make a long story short, let me tell you that I went ahead to graduate from Butler, cum laude, from Christian Theological Seminary, magma cum laude, and to get my masters degree. In the fall of 1978 I decided to hit the books again, and a year and a half later I received my Doctor of Ministries degree from Drew University.

I am not telling you all of this in order to point out what a neat guy Ralph is. I know far better than that. As a matter of fact, whatever pride I have is radically diminished by my knowledge that many other so-called handicapped persons have done the same sort of thing that I have. Look at any college graduating class. I'll bet that you will see handicapped students in the front ranks of it.

As I evaluate the situation, there is a very simple explanation. The good Lord puts into each one of us a ton of potential, and most of us only manage to use a few ounces of it. We have bundles of possibilities within us, but we are usually content to squeeze out just about as much as we need in order to get along. The majority of our potential is left to rot away and disintegrate within us.

But perhaps, just perhaps, something happens that turns us on and causes us to call forth some of the boundless possibilities that have been going to waste within us. It happened for me. A thing called blindness, a force called fear, they energized powers that I had never discovered within myself, and I was amazed by my accomplishments. This same sort of thing has happened to many, many handicapped individuals.

I told you a little while ago about a prayer that I have for my daughter and for those who are close to me. Let me confess that there is a second stanza to my prayer. "Lord, may something happen that will turn them on to the potentials that are within them. I pray that it won't be blindness or anything as terrible as that, but I pray even more fervently that it will happen. Let them be turned on and enable them to profitably employ the vast treasury of resources that you have placed within them."

In the eighth chapter of Romans Paul has written a phrase that summarizes many of my thoughts. He has said, "For I am sure that neither death, nor life, nor angels, nor principalities, nor things present, nor things to come, nor powers, nor height, nor depth, nor anything else in all creation, will be able to separate us from the love of God in Christ Jesus our Lord." If I may be permitted to change the language a bit, may I tell you that neither blindness, nor deafness, nor cancer, nor diabetes, nor the tragedy of early illness, nor the feebleness that is brought on by advancing years, nothing within us or beyond us can separate us from the love of God that Jesus Christ has made known to us. By the grace of God you can't keep a good man down.

How can I know the mind of God?
I can read great books and think deep thoughts,
But how can I separate God's voice from those of the clamoring
    chorus?
    I hear the siren song of tradition;
    My listening is filled with the voices of my world and colored by
        the tones of my own desires;
    And in the babble I cannot differentiate between the mortal and the
        divine.
The prophet declares the mind of God;
He has no questions, no uncertainties concerning the divine intent;
But how can I know who is truly prophetic, or who is just a loud and
    irresponsible trumpet?
    How can I know the mind of God?
    I can test my apprehensions upon the anvil of circumstance,
    And I can listen for the word that rings true above all others;
And then my final resource is a prayer:
"O God, reveal a fragment of Yourself to me,
And help me in the insecurity of faith to know that it is You."

Hear The Word
of the Lord

Our study group came together for the first time in late August of 1979. We met at an Indianapolis retreat center and spent three intensive days with a member of the Drew University faculty who had been flown in for the event. It was during this initial study meeting that I found myself confronted with a major problem.

The university's faculty representative told our group that each of us was to spend his second year of doctoral study conducting and writing up a special professional project in his church. Each project was to be undergirded by theological understanding and thoughtful consideration, but each was to be centrally related to the student's own ministry within the bounds of his congregation. The project paper which would rise from each of our efforts was not to be an ivory tower instrument. It was to be well-rooted in the practice of ministry and to be of value both to the student and to his congregation.

I have always thought of myself as a preacher and have dreamed of the day when I might be able to instruct seminarians in the art of homiletics. For this reason my mind began to reach out and to consider the variety of possibilities that I had regarding a study centered about preaching. I was full of ideas as our three-day session ended and as I began the drive home in company with two other students. We shared our thoughts as we drove, and at that moment I was confronted with an entirely new thought.

I suddenly realized that any Christian minister could enter into a study and write a paper concerning preaching. Undoubtedly, thousands upon thousands had. In regard to homiletics it would be hard, indeed, for me to say anything that was new or that would be considered as a real contribution to Christian scholarship and ministry. After all, the very fact that a minister is often regarded as a "preacher" speaks volumes concerning the focus that has been placed upon homiletics, seemingly since the beginning of time.

I wanted to make some sort of contribution. As we drove and talked, I realized that I wanted my doctoral efforts to be of some value to the Christian community of today and tomorrow. I began to ask myself questions regarding the experiences and opportunities that were uniquely mine. It was at this point that I made a tentative commitment to some sort of study that would measure and give theological meaning to the value of handicap, and specifically blindness, in the Christian ministry.

At that time I was operating from a hunch that very little had been said and written regarding the place of handicapped persons in ministry. A trip to a local seminary's library quickly confirmed my suspicions. There were plenty of books about handicaps on the shelves. Virtually all of these, however, dealt with the ways in which the church and community could understand handicaps and be of assistance to the handicapped. I found absolutely nothing regarding the vital concern of the place that handicapped persons might have in ministering to society. As I considered the vacuum of study and of writing related to the role that handicapped people have in serving others, I knew that I had a project. I would be blazing new trails and would be making crucial steps into fresh territory.

As a background to my proposed study, I had the solid belief that my personal blindness had not greatly hampered, and that it may well have helped, my own life in ministry. As I have told you in an earlier chapter, I was also aware of testimony being given by well-meaning social workers to the effect that sightless persons could not be expected to be ministers, if for no other reason, because they could not drive autos. Questions of all sorts began to race through my fascinated mind. What was the Church's historical position regarding handicap in ministry? What Biblical foundations were there for the belief that handicap might even be a source of strength? What did the understandings of qualified social workers have to offer by way of insight? Were there other blind and otherwise handicapped persons who shared experiences similar to mine? As my mind wandered in this line of thought, I found myself wondering if my own congregation shared my perceptions and did not look upon my lack of sight as a horrendous handicap. My list of questions stretched on and on. I set myself upon the course of finding answers for them.

Anyone who wishes to wade through the desert-dry pages of a

doctoral study is welcome to read my final project paper: *The Impact Of My Physical Blindness Upon My Ministry At The Burlington United Methodist Church.* It is available through University Microfilms of Ann Arbor, Michigan. In this chapter I want to lift from my paper a few of the exciting understandings that came to me in my year of examination and reflection. I will color these perceptions with some personal illustrations.

I was amazed to discover that the religious community has historically held a mixed and, really a rather, negative view towards handicapped persons serving in the ranks of the clergy. Many Judeo-Christian attitudes were codified and shaped by references in Leviticus which declare against the possibility of "marred" persons serving as priests of the Lord. Although I had been a minister for many years, I had never read these texts. One of them (Leviticus 21:16-23 RSV) is quoted here.

> *And the Lord said to Moses, "Say to Aaron, None of your descendants throughout their generations who has a blemish may approach to offer the bread of his God. For no one who has a blemish shall draw near, a man blind or lame, or one who has a mutilated face or a limb too long, or a man who has an injured foot or an injured hand, or a hunchback, or a dwarf, or a man with a defect in his sight or an itching disease or scabs or crushed testicles; no man of the descendants of Aaron the priest who has a blemish shall come near to offer the Lord's offerings by fire; since he has a blemish, he shall not come near to offer the bread of his God. He may eat the bread of his God, both of the most holy and of the holy things, but he shall not come near the veil or approach the altar, because he has a blemish, that he may not profane my sanctuaries; for I am the Lord who sanctify them."*

The attitude that a priest should not in any way be marred is, I suppose, in harmony with the belief that sacrificial animals should be perfect in every way. It seems to rise from the notion that the Lord should receive only "the best," and it defines "the best" in strictly physical terms.

I think that I understand the problem that is associated with this Levitical concern. It is reflected in a recent newspaper clipping telling of a sign that was seen outside a Wisconsin church: "There will be no faith healing services this evening due to the illness of the pastor."

How, in fact, can a blind man preach the Gospel of Him who caused the blind to see, or a crippled person speak out in behalf of Him who said, "Take up your bed and walk?" Is it any wonder that the Church has been slow to open the doors of ministry to the handicapped?

There is another theological and Biblical theme that must now be considered. It is a theme that was embodied by Jesus, Himself, and was crucial to St. Paul, who was certainly a principal force in the development of the early Church. I speak of the theme of suffering and the revelation that it is he who is hurt that most readily serves as an agency for divine grace.

Christians see the entire 53rd chapter of Isaiah as a prophetic anticipation of the suffering and death of the Christ. Let's think of some of the words: "He was wounded for our transgressions; He was bruised for our iniquities . . . The Lord has laid on Him the iniquity of us all . . . With His stripes we are healed." Those who stood before the cross and jeered, insulted Jesus with the same words that modern cynics might direct to the faith healer who is sick. They said: "If you are really the Christ, come down from the cross . . . He saved others; He can not save Himself." (Matthew 27)

It is hard for us to explain exactly how Jesus' suffering is beneficial to us. Theology books are filled with all sorts of interpretations of what we call "the atonement." The fact is that the Son of God, who according to our measure was perfect, suffered terribly and died. In a strange way we have found healing because of His wounds.

It was the same with Paul, the apostle. During the course of his life in ministry he was jailed, whipped, stoned, shipwrecked, and God only knows what else. He was apparently a weak man physically because he tells us that he suffered from a "thorn in the flesh." No one knows for sure what that "thorn" was for Paul. Some speculate that it was epilepsy; others believe it may have been a problem with vision. We are not sure what Paul's problem was; however, it was evidently some sort of physical malady. The point that I am making is this: writing in regard to all of these problems, Paul said that the Lord told him: " 'My grace is sufficient for you, for my power is made perfect in weakness.' " (2 Corinthians 12:9) The apostle saw the fact that he was weak to be the true sign of God's strength working within him.

Put it this way. If you and I should be at the scene of a fire and see a big, strapping fireman come out the door carrying an extraordinarily heavy piece of furniture, we might point at him and say "Gee!" If, on the other hand, we should see the same piece of furniture being brought out by a five-foot-four, 120-pound teen-ager, we would shake our heads in disbelief and wonder. We would find ourselves asking where on earth the little guy managed to get all of his strength. Paul used his weakness to demonstrate where in heaven his source of ability was.

As centuries have passed, the Church has done much to lead the way for the inclusion of handicapped persons in ordinary life. In its best moments it has listened to its own voice and has made room for those who are physically handicapped to step into the ranks of its ministers. I suspect, though, that the Church has never been fully aware of the strengths and possibilities that its handicapped pastors bring to their practice of ministry.

I began to sense that possibility when I was a student in college. After lunch I would go upstairs in our fraternity house and would flop out on a bed for a few minutes rest. Time after time I found John, or Cal, or one of the other guys coming up to join me and starting to share the troubles of their lives. I'll never forget the sunny after-noon when I was studying physics with Ted. We were working our way through a chapter on electrical theory when Ted suddenly threw the book down and blurted out, "Let's face it, Ralph; I'm going to go to hell." You can believe that a lot of conversation followed that remark.

It was common for my fraternity brothers to open up to me con-cerning their many problems and deep questions. They seemed to feel that I knew what life's difficulties were all about, and that I would be able to understand them. Their openness was one of the several factors that caused me to begin thinking of the pastorate.

Those who have come to my office for counseling have told me many things about the ways that my lack of sight has affected them. One lady told me that she was disconcerted when she realized that her carefully applied make up wasn't impressing me a bit. She had put it on in order to camouflage her hurts and insecurity. When she realized that her pretense wasn't affecting me she got down to brass tacks in a hurry and started telling me about all of her difficulties.

Another counselee remarked that my not seeing her gave her the freedom to turn red in the face, to cry, or to express her pent-up feel-ings however she cared to. She said that, had I been looking at her, it would have been much harder for her to be honest with me or with herself.

At the beginning of this chapter I mentioned our doctoral study group. After our two-year expedition into new knowledge was over, one of the group's members told me that there were several times when he was tempted to give up and quit. "Whenever I felt that way," he said, "I thought of you and figured that if you could do it, I surely could too." Let me be quick to say that I don't really like being used as a model. God only knows that there are far too many times when my own weakness and human frailties are appallingly evident. (Ask my family; they will tell all.) I accept the fact, though, that there are times when others do find courage and faith from their view of me. If my life is able to convey a sense of grace and possibility, I am deeply grateful. When my humanity shows through too vividly, I can only beg for understanding.

Let me be clear and openly confess that this preacher is totally capable of thinking unkind thoughts and of muttering unspeakable words, when he stubs his bare toe while on the way to the bathroom or falls over his dog who is asleep in the bedroom doorway. He suspects that the Lord understands, and he hopes that others do too.

There are other ways in which blindness has enhanced my ministry. I have already told you that I have never been accused of reading a sermon. I talk to people directly when I preach, and I believe that they like it. There are, of course, some unusual dynamics on the job when a sightless pastor is in the pulpit. People have to get used to the idea that the minister may not know if they go to sleep during the sermon. During the last week that I spent in a former parish, two sisters who were old enough to know better confessed that they wouldn't know how to act in front of a preacher who could see them sitting in the back row of the church talking to one another. I chose to tell them that they are free people who are not accountable to me as some sort of high-blown authority figure. I reminded them that their responsibility is to themselves and to God. In that moment I hope that I taught a very important and often forgotten lesson.

As I write this page, I am preparing to leave my typewriter and get properly dressed for a wedding. I fancy that I know the couple at least as well as most pastors do, and that they feel a special closeness to me. I will not be reading the liturgy this evening. We will not be separated by a book as I bring them together as husband and wife, a new family in God's world. Because of the intimacy allowed by our direct relationship this evening, I believe that the wedding will have a unique quality.

What I have been telling you is theoretical and subjective. My words rise from Biblical speculation and out of my own view of my life and work. I was aware of this problem as I ventured into my study, and I concluded that I must put theory and subjectivity to the test by examining the apprehensions of my own congregation which I, at that time, had served as pastor for nearly six years.

I may be blind, but I am most certainly not dumb. I knew at the beginning of my study that I couldn't go to members of my congregation and ask them what they thought about my blindness. Under such circumstances, folks would have told me what they thought I wanted to hear and not necessarily what they, themselves, thought and believed. What I wanted was an honest measuring of my own congregation's attitudes towards my lack of sight. For this reason I selected and trained a highly qualified committee that would go into our church community with a carefully prepared questionnaire. I knew that even a procedure such as this would still reflect a measure of prejudice. I felt, though, it would do the job fairly well.

The committee was chosen, and the questionnaire was prepared. Our congregation was properly polled, and the results were brought back to me. I was amazed and gratified by the response.

When given a chance to speculate about blindness, the persons who knew me best continued to raise questions about the limitations that my sightlessness must lay upon my ministry. When confronted with individual situations, though, and when asked what effect my lack of vision had upon them in the circumstances of weddings, funerals, baptisms, hospital visits, sermons, and the great variety of specific ways in which they met me pastorally, my congregation declared that my blindness actually enhanced my ministry. They seemed to say that it caused my preaching to be more personal, and my funeral services to be more sensitive and intimate. They seemed to feel that I shared in the mixture of suffering and faith and gave them a new quality of hope as I visited with them in the hospital. They did far more than report that my lack of sight made little difference to them; they affirmed that it was a source of strength for them. A person reading the summary of our survey might well conclude that it would be a good thing for all ministers to be blind.

I am including the tables which summarize the results of my questionnaire and will allow them to speak for themselves. If you are not interested in statistics, you can skip these tables and continue with my narrative.

QUESTIONNAIRE RESPONSE SUMMARY

I. General Attitudes

Most of the following questions can be answered with a single number based on a scale of 1 to 10. Circle the number that reflects your response.

1. When I first thought of a blind minister as pastor of my church I was (1, very worried, to 10, very enthusiastic):

(1,	2,	3,	4,	5,	6,	7,	8,	9,	10)	*AV
10	4	8	14	56	20	12	12	4	7	5.33

2. When I first met Rev. Karstedt, my feelings about his blindness were (1, no feeling, to 10, strong feeling):

(1,	2,	3,	4,	5,	6,	7,	8,	9,	10)	*AV
7	5	7	9	41	17	14	21	6	20	6.01

3. When I met him, my thoughts regarding his blindness were (1, deeply bothered, to 10, excited and inspired):

(1,	2,	3,	4,	5,	6,	7,	8,	9,	10)	*AV
3	5	2	7	28	22	25	23	8	27	6.80

4. When I spoke to others, especially those outside of our church family about him, I (1, avoided speaking of his blindness or apologized for it, to 10, spoke of it with excitement):

(1,	2,	3,	4,	5,	6,	7,	8,	9,	10)	*AV
2	0	1	2	22	11	11	34	21	43	7.87

5. I have now known Rev. Karstedt for _____ years. [Answers to this question are not relevant as summarized information.]

6. I now think of his blindness (1, frequently, to 10, seldom):

1,	2,	3,	4,	5,	6,	7,	8,	9,	10)	*AV
5	2	4	1	14	4	8	21	29	59	8.12

7. My feelings now about his blindness are (1, bothered, to 10, inspired):

(1,	2,	3,	4,	5,	6,	7,	8,	9,	10)	*AV
0	2	2	2	22	10	6	18	20	65	8.19

8. In regard to him being minister of my church, I now think of his blindness as (1, a liability, to 10, an asset):

(1,	2,	3,	4,	5,	6,	7,	8,	9,	10)	*AV
0	0	3	4	33	19	11	22	13	44	7.53

9. When speaking to friends about my minister, I (1, often refer to his blindness, to 10, seldom mention it):

(1,	2,	3,	4,	5,	6,	7,	8,	9,	10	*AV
16	3	11	7	26	9	14	15	12	31	6.27

10. When speaking to friends about his blindness, I express:

    a. sorrow for him   1
    b. pride in him   90
    c. both sorrow and pride   44
    d. other _____   11

*AV = means average response.

II. Pastoral Encounters

In the following items, place a check at the left of those lines that apply to you. At the right of each of the checked lines give a numerical score (−5 to +5). The score should indicate the effect that our pastor's blindness had upon you in each event listed. (−5, greatly hampered; 0, made no difference; +5, greatly helped):

	*AV	−5	−4	−3	−2	−1	0	+1	+2	+3	+4	+5
11. funeral of family member	2.21						25	1	2	3	4	17
12. funeral service you attended	1.75						38	1	2	5	7	15
13. counseling with you	2.22				1		14	2	4	4	1	13
14. wedding of yours or of a close family member	2.35					1	19	2		4	5	15
15. wedding you attended	1.53						30	1		4	1	11
16. Baptism of you or of a family member	2.13	1			1		15		3	2	4	12
17. Baptism that you witnessed	1.77	1		1	2	2	38	2	3	5	4	24
18. received into membership of church (you or family member)	2.17						22	2	1	5	2	15
19. visited you in your home	1.84						47	4	2	3	6	23
20. visited in hospital (you or family member)	2.64			1		2	25	2	2	3	14	27
21. preaching	2.32	1			1		53	4	8	8	18	40
22. worship leadership	2.00					1	45	1	7	5	10	23
23. other (Please indicate)	3.56				1					2	2	4

24. Please relate specific information regarding your feelings and experiences regarding any of the above. Staying with the issue of our minister's blindness, be as thoughtful and complete as you can. [Answers to this question were varied and can not be summarized.] *AV = means average response.

III. Life Changes

Consider the items below and check on the left those which apply to you and in which Rev. Karstedt played a significant part. On the right indicate by number score the extent to which Rev. Karstedt's blindness related to the event. (−5, greatly hampered, 0, made no difference, +5, greatly helped):

	*AV	−5	−4	−3	−2	−1	0	+1	+2	+3	+4	+5
25. entered church membership	1.96						13	1	1	2		8
26. became more active in church participation	1.77	.					14	2	5	2	3	5
27. took new job in church	1.57						18	1	1	3		7
28. brought friend or relative into church relationship	1.75						8		4			4
29. made major life decision (please indicate) 2.29							7		1			6

In numbers 30 and 31 indicate (on a scale from 1 to 10) that his blindness: (1, contributed significantly to the event, to 10, had no relevance to the event).

	*AV	1	2	3	4	5	6	7	8	9	10
30. relinquished church job	9.65					1				1	15
31. became less active in church participation	9.58				1					2	16

*AV = means average response.

Let me take a moment to tell you about Maude. I met her when I visited her in the hospital during the first year of my ministry in the parish. When I came to the door of her room, I heard her giving thunder to a couple of poor nurses who were trying to help her and were bewildered by her very vocal and physical resistance to being hospitalized. They scooted into the hall with a whispered word of thanks when they saw me entering Maude's room. Then Maude looked up and saw me. With a hostile tone remaining in her voice, she glared at me and barked: "And I suppose you want me to go to heaven!" I commented that she had a pretty good idea, but that there really wasn't any hurry. That's how I got to know Maude.

I mention this woman now, because one of my interviewers told me that Maude was really bothered by my blindness. She said that it really made her uncomfortable and that she often wondered if I were in pain. As I heard the account I found myself wondering if my eyes were putting Maude in touch with her own pain and loneliness. I suspected that I might be forcing her to a new sort of self-understanding and acceptance.

The next part of my story is very factual but is written quite tentatively. Maude died a year or so after she had been interviewed. It turned out that she had recently revised her will and that she had left a substantial part of her estate to our church. I still am not sure how this event should be interpreted. Perhaps she would have changed her will so as to include the church whether I was or was not on the scene. Perhaps the factors that caused her to write her new will were totally separate from who I was. Perhaps my blindness forced her to look at herself and reevaluate the priorities of her life. Her voice was, in fact, one of the few negative ones that were raised, and she did, after the time of the questionnaire, make a very significant change in her expressed values. I leave you to reach your own conclusions.

My mind goes back to the last Sunday that I spent at the pastorate of a former church. Mrs. B. came to me to express her appreciation. She said that she was grateful that her children had had the opportunity to know me. She thought that I had brought a profound impact upon their lives.

The effects that my blindness were reported to have brought to my ministry seemed to fit into one of three different categories. Let me mention each of them briefly.

Many persons saw my weakness as a human agency through which God's healing love can be manifested. I almost choke as I write these words, because I know that a blind person is not an apparent example of one who has been healed. Too often we associate healing with physical changes and too seldom do we recognize the full dynamics of the way God works within us. I sometimes am convinced that pragmatic lay persons have a clearer understanding of life's full panoply than do pastors. Every lay person knows what it is to have a fervent prayer apparently unanswered. Such a person does not have to interpret his experiences in terms of preset theology. He or she does not have to continue to talk about the healing that God can offer "if only we believe." There is the simple and obvious acceptance of the fact that physical healing has not come, and then there is the realization that a new sense of strength is with the wounded. When a handicapped pastor comes on the scene, he authenticates the common person's experience and helps such a person to realize that the healing grace of God takes many forms.

Closely associated with this concept is the understanding that, as a blind pastor, I force persons to confront their own humanity. You and I live in a culture when youth and sparkling health have practically been deified. Everyone wants to seem as spry and energetic as the wonderful young people who pose for magazine ads and bounce into the center of our TV screens. We dye our hair (or cover our bald spots), lie about our age, and hesitate to tell anyone (perhaps ourselves especially) about the onset of creaking joints and faltering powers. Recall my mention of Maude, who found herself hurting as she looked upon my frailty. When a respected member of the community appears as a handicapped one, he pushes people to consider his humanity and their own too. It is as though he says, "Look at me; I am imperfect, and that's okay. Your imperfection and brokenness is okay too. Let's stop kidding ourselves and be part of the human race together."

Underlying the other two concepts is the thought that a "wounded healer" sort of pastor offers an example which seems to say, "If I can do it, you can too." As I wrote earlier, this sort of example is very dangerous. When a person sets himself up in an exemplary way, he makes it very hard to have continuing problems. When he says, "Look at me; see how well I handle tough situations," he puts himself in the position of not daring to fail or falter before the public eye. Please understand that there is no real virtue in falling on your face. The fact is, though, that an exemplary person must be willing to take quite a few public tumbles. It is the only way that he can retain credibility before others.

I am reminded of a blind friend who recently attended a hockey game in Indianapolis. Between the periods Carl decided that he needed a trip to the men's room. Although friends sitting beside him offered to take him to the appropriate place, Carl announced that he could do it for himself, thank you. He took off with white cane tapping before him. He went down the steps and out into the main hall of the arena. He made a proper turn towards the rest rooms and was quite pleased with himself as he swung open the door of the room out of which there came the sound of functioning plumbing. His pleasure was brought to a grinding halt when a number of raised feminine voices told him that he had made one small mistake.

It is to Carl's credit that he is able to tell the story of this embarrassing blunder. It is to the credit of any of us who is able to face up to his own weaknesses. Accepting our humanity is a big part of living successfully. It authenticates us as real people.

I commenced this chapter telling you about my embarkation upon a project to measure the effect of my blindness upon ministry. From time to time I have substituted the word "handicapped" for that of "blind." As my thoughts have progressed, a new revelation has been looming before me with increasing clarity.

Isn't there a sense in which we are all handicapped? After all, a handicap is no more or less than a limitation that is imposed upon us. Some are limited because of lack of sight, or sound, or the ability to move legs or hands. Others are limited by their tempers, or their financial circumstances, or the bald spots upon their heads.

May I add a parenthetical comment that I often think of my baldness as a real handicap. Every time I go bike riding with my wife, I come home with a sunburned dome. It's really tough combing the few hairs that are left when you have to rake the comb across the surface of a good burn. That's what I call a real handicap.

Don't let me trivialize tough problems. Real handicap is very serious. Let me insist, though, that in some sense we all are among the ranks of the wounded and the afflicted. My point is that our limitations, no matter what, do not need to limit us. They can be agencies for grace and strength. I asked my congregation, and they told me that it is so.

Do you remember the old spiritual that speaks of the "Dry Bones" that are going to rise again? Each verse ends with the phrase, "Now hear the word of the Lord." The word of the Lord is that the very bones that represent our mortality and defeat can rise up and enable us to walk with dignity and strength. I will not be so stupid as to thank God for having made me blind. As a matter of fact, I don't believe that He did, but that's a different story. I am convinced, though, that my blindness has become a central force in the developing of Ralph and in the integrity and validity of my life and ministry.

Truly the very bones of apparent weakness and failure have become the frame upon which my continuing life stands. "Now hear the word of the Lord." I humbly join the throngs who say "Amen."

I sit down to write and know
    That new thoughts will soon flow through my moving fingers,
    And that my words shall trace out patterns of images and ideas
    Of which my imagination has now only the tiniest conception.
I commence a new day with the knowledge
    That I cannot control its direction and quality,
    For the day is like a poem waiting to be written,
    And I can only guess at its conclusion.
Yet I know that a flow of thought will emerge from my poetic mind,
    And I also understand that my day is waiting to be lived,
    So I set myself to the penmanship of this day
    And am spellbound by the drama that I describe.
Come, share with me the poetry of this fresh day,
    For you and I must write the verse together,
    Since life is a stanza written by countless pens,
    And you and I now share the writing.

Come Walk With Me

An over-used saying tells us that we can never truly understand another person unless we have walked in his sandals. I am sure that there must be truth in these words. When we place our feet in the sandals of someone else, we are surely best able to experience that person's joys and sorrows, loves and hates, faith and fears, and athlete's foot too.

I am now at the beginning of a new day in the life of me. Breakfast is over, and I have just slipped into my office and taken my place in my comfortable chair. My mind is beginning to gain some sort of focus, and I am ready to launch into the drama and boredom of a January Friday. Would you like to join me? Perhaps you can begin to see the beauty, humor, and tragedy of life as I see it. Welcome to this "today" of our lives.

It is a little hard for me to know exactly what thoughts and activities I should share with you so that you can be with me in this day. It would be foolish and blatantly impossible for me to describe every breath I breathe, every thought I think, and every step I take during the course of twenty-four hours. I must extrapolate from the continuum of experience those specific images and happenings that can help you to walk in my shoes (I don't like sandals) and see life through the blank visual perspective of my plastic eyes. I know that this venture of description will be a bit tough for me, because I must remember that I have come to accept as commonplace a host of thoughts and activities that would be so strange as to seem bizarre to you.

Can you accept the fact that nothing unusual transpired in the hour or so that preceded my trip to the office? There is really no drama in the business of shaving a face or brushing a set of teeth. Neither is the process of filling and consuming a bowl of cereal especially exciting. You may want to disagree with me on this point, for you may be bothered by the notion of bringing a blade razor close to your face or of attempting to pour milk into a bowl while under the conditions of a total blackout. Let me assure you that the scare in these activities is natural for one who is attempting such tricks for the first time. It doesn't take long to conquer routine problems, though, and activities such as these quickly become very unremarkable.

Take the matter of filling a coffee cup. My friends will smile as they read this paragraph, for they well know that coffee is a near addiction to me. The first time you try to fill a cup without being able to see it, you will probably have some problems. You may miss hitting the cup in the first place. Your probable mistake is that of not knowing when to "say when." The writer of the Psalms may think that it's pretty nice to have a cup that runneth over, but if you're blind and the coffee is both messy and hot, you may need a little convincing. Here's how you solve the problem. Let one finger of your left hand rest just over the inside edge of the cup as you pour the brew with your right. (Reverse the process if you are left-handed.) The hotness that rises up to touch your finger will quickly tell you when to shut off the flow. Repeat the process a few times so that you can toughen up your nearly scalded finger tip, and coffee pouring has become a non-issue.

In a similar way there are successful ways for conquering the challenges that are imposed by razors, neckties, and money exchanging. Each is in its own way interesting, but none is really noteworthy. Let's leave such commonplace matters behind us, step out of my house, and walk across to the church.

I personally use a cane when I walk. One thing that my poodle is not is a guide dog. If I left guidance up to Mr. French, he and I would end up in the next block sniffing after a cat. As you and I walk from my house to the nearby church, then, I have cane in hand.

As long as there is a well-paved and predictable sidewalk in front of us, I have no problems. If I swing the cane in front of me from right to left and left to right, it will help me know the location of the walk's edges and also give warning of curbs, bicycles, and other obstacles that may be in the way. The only problem that I have in reaching our church is imposed by a large graveled parking lot. There is absolutely no way that I can use my cane to gain orientation when it touches gravel, no matter where and when I swing it. As I enter the parking lot, I must set a course and stick to it. My cane will tell me when I reach the sidewalk on the other side.

The trip across that parking lot shouldn't be hard. After all, if my course is off by a degree or two I should still come up against the walk that surrounds the church. A church is pretty big, and it's hard to miss. I must confess, though, that I have missed it on a few occasions. At those times when my compass has really been out of whack, I have been very grateful for an observant neighbor (if I were using alliteration, I would say "nosey") who watches my every trip to make sure that I won't fall off the edge of the world.

Now I am at the church. Mr. French is snoozing at my feet, and my day has begun. For the past hour I have been reading from a fascinating book. It is Gordan W. Prang's definitive history of Pearl Harbor entitled, *At Dawn We Slept*. I like to read different kinds of books during my first hour in the office. Some days it will be the Bible. Some days it will be biography. Today it is history. These books help me to energize my mind, and give me the opportunity to interpret my perspectives in constantly changing settings.

You may well be more interested in how I am reading than you are in what I am reading. With the help of a Talking Book machine that has been supplied me by Uncle Sam, I am reading through my ears. I often involve myself in hand activity as I read. I am one preacher who does not mind folding worship bulletins and preparing newsletters for mailing. It sometimes helps me to have my fingers busy while my mind is active. Besides I can earn double pay this way.

It is now 9:00 a.m., the hour when most people think that it is respectable to phone an office. My phone is ringing now. This call is related to our camp for retarded people. I have been privileged to serve as chairperson for the committee that oversees it. The committee also has responsibility for our conference's camping activities in behalf of the deaf and the blind. I can never put too much time into such an enterprise. Its value is beyond measure.

My phone will probably be hot for the next hour or so. I have learned to use it extensively. Ma Bell's ads telling me that "I can let my fingers do the walking," and I may "reach out and touch someone" are admonitions that I have taken very seriously. I may not be able to drive, but I can cover lots of territory in a hurry by way of the telephone. Friends tell me that I am a walking phone directory too. Such a reputation can sometimes be a nuisance. I actually have one or two persons who will ring me up to get a phone number that may not be printed in the directory. After all, they would have to pay if they called information.

It's nearly 11:00 a.m., and on Friday morning that means initial sermon time. I never write a sermon manuscript. If I had 20/20 vision, I would still not write one. Written texts are intended for visual reading. They use a complex language form that is not well-suited to the ear of the listener. I "talk out" my sermons with what I call an oral manuscript. This is how it works.

Early in the week I have committed myself to a basic sermon idea. If you want to know how that comes about, ask me in the next chapter. As the week progresses, I have collected a variety of ideas and illustrations concerning the message. I have also worked out a basic outline. On Friday morning (Saturday if I am totally lazy) I commence the process of putting it all together. I do it by simply sitting behind my desk and talking the sermon through. I don't worry about grammatical blunders and verbal effects at this time; I simply start talking through the sermon following the outline of thought that I have already worked out. I'll do this twice on Friday and will go through the process about three times more on Saturday morning. Each time I will arrange and refine my words a bit. Always I will be listening to myself and be asking the questions: "Is this what I want to say? Is this the best way to say it?" Please understand that I am not memorizing the sermon. What I am doing is discovering what I want to say by listening to myself. I am also giving myself the assurance that I have in hand the language necessary to express my thoughts.

There are two things that I never do as I move through this sort of sermon preparation. I never tape record my words so as to listen to the replay before Sunday. There is nothing more rigid and dull than a sermon that is being "practiced." If I were to hear a tape of my preparations, I would be so appalled by my stiffness and awkwardness that I would never preach again. A sermon is more than a carefully prepared discourse. It is a verbal presentation that serves as a thought bridge connecting a pastor and the people of the congregation. A sermon needs live listeners in order to make it live. The only recording that I ever listen to is that of the live sermon that is actually presented at the 9:30 hour on Sunday morning.

The other thing that I never do in the process of preparation is to run through the message from behind the pulpit out in the sanctuary. I want my preaching in the sanctuary to be a "once and for real" experience. My preaching would tend to be sterile if I allowed the sanctuary to be anything but fresh and real. When the worship hour comes, I meet my congregation and the vital spark of God's Spirit and allow my preaching to have an attitude of newness. For me this is important.

There is only one person other than myself who ever hears one of my sermons before the time of preaching. Our faithful janitor often hears major parts of my messages as she cleans the church. She sometimes kids me and tells me that she won't need to come to church since she has heard the sermon already. I always tell her that she missed the best part while she was emptying the wastebasket.

My sermon is beginning to take shape in my mind, when suddenly there is a tap on my door. "Pardon me," says an unseen voice, "Is the pastor in?" It is my friend, David (I jokingly call him King David), come to join me for lunch. David is minister of a neighboring church. He and I have been good friends for years. We share lunch frequently and use our mealtimes to exchange ideas. As we begin walking the two blocks between my church and the local restaurant, I tell him about my sermon development. He tosses in an insight that had gotten past me. The hour is already worthwhile.

For me, eating lunch with others is a regular occurrence. I have a list of fellow pastors and close friends with whom I like to share my noon hours. I am so regular a visitor at our restaurant that I pull back the chain that closes off the normally unused dining section so that I can get away from the smoke and clamor of the noisy lunchroom. The waitresses smile at me indulgently and come in my direction with a full cup of coffee.

I guess that I am a people type of person. I simply enjoy being with others. After the relative isolation in an "ivory tower" office, I am more than ready to become social. More than this, I need persons on whom I can test my ideas. I am an arguer. No matter what someone says, I will subconsciously move to the opposite side of the debate. I firmly believe that any notion needs to be tried and tested before it should be accepted. Hence, lunch time conversation is often exciting.

There may be a special sense in which my lack of sight feeds the need for noontime socializing. I am very much aware that I do not manage to read all of the professional magazines and periodicals that fill my daily mail. My wife and I read a good amount of mail together, but the publications are often beyond the limits of our time. I manage to get in touch with many of the magazines' major themes through my luncheon conversations. Dave, Don, or Joe will ask me about a particularly stimulating item that they have read. My immediate response is to say, "Tell me."

Ever since my college days I have known that interchanges such as these can be very helpful. I have also known that they are beneficial to my friends as much or more than they are to me.

Back in college I always managed to recruit one or two volunteers who would study each course with me. They would read the texts aloud, and we would discuss them at length. We always studied for finals using a combination of their notes and my memory.

At first I felt a bit guilty because I was imposing upon friends for a great deal of their time and energy. It took them, for example, at least twice as long to read a book out loud as it would have were they reading silently. A couple of our professors put me straight in regard to the matter of guilt. They told me that my helpers consistently raised their own grades by at least one point. B students would get A's; C students would bring home B's, etc. I quickly realized that the interchanging of our ideas was the key to personal growth for all of us. I remain convinced that I bring at least as much to such meetings as do my friends. Since they keep on coming, I suspect that they share my point of view.

I flip open my watch and notice that it is five minutes until 1:00. My watch is obviously an old-fashioned one with hands. Were I using a digital, I would have reported 12:55. At this writing Braille watches have not come out as digitals. I tell time by flipping up the watch cover and feeling the position of the hands. Raised dots mark the hours and make the task simple.

It is time for a quick dash back to the church, because I have a 1:00 appointment with Joyce. Joyce is one of several parishioners who have agreed to assist me once every month or so by going with me on pastoral calls. I normally go out about two afternoons a week with people like her. This afternoon we will visit a nursing home and stop in to inspect a brand new baby and to share in the wonder of new life with her parents. It will be an enjoyable afternoon.

I am sometimes asked how it works to have parishioners accompany me on most of my pastoral calling. I answer by saying that results are surprisingly good. A lay person traveling with me projects the image of a caring church. I am the pastor; I am paid to make calls. When a volunteer accompanies me, that person represents the dedication of a congregation. It casts an atmosphere of warmth upon the events of the visit.

I must be honest and say that people whom I am visiting rarely raise touchy personal issues when I am accompanied by another. I know this and often tell folks that they are invited to come to my office to discuss intimate concerns. What I am trying to do in my home visits is to create relationship. I come, in this case with Joyce, and we represent a caring God and church. A person who comes to know me in such a way will find it easy to move from the experience of our visit to that of ringing my phone and saying, "Ralph, may I stop in for a couple of minutes tomorrow?"

The presence of my driving companions always brings a non-professional aura to my visiting. How can I forget the time in a Marion, Indiana, nursing home when Inda got a pitcher and watered the patient's artificial plant? Speaking of Inda, I must tell you that after I left the church where she worshiped, I got a letter from her that made my heart sing. She wrote that she had missed sharing with me in our visits and that she had decided that she wasn't just going to sit at home by herself. She had just started driving to the hospitals and nursing homes without the preacher. My pastoral spirit feels that her letter spelled out a real success story.

I think of the many persons who are now my driving helpers. Several of them have previously been recipients of my calls. They, themselves, have been hospitalized and visited by me, or they have had family members who have experienced the warmth of such caring. After their personal crisis, they have phoned to ask if they, too, can help.

The afternoon is getting late, and it is time for visiting to come to an end. Mrs. Jones doesn't really appreciate a visit when she is trying to prepare supper. Joyce lets me off at the house, and I give her a big thank you. The appreciation, augmented by her own sense of accomplishment, is the only pay that she will get for this day. What more pay does a person need?

As I take off my shoes and wiggle my weary toes, I find myself wondering what the evening will be like. If it were June or July I would probably be hurting for a bike ride. My wife and I have been ardent bikers for many years. We have two tandems in our garage, one for slow local riding, and a sleek job that we use when we really hit the roads. A nice fifteen-miler would feel great right now, but it's not a good idea when we have three inches of snow on the ground.

Before going further, let me tell you a thing or two about being the back end on a tandem bike. In the first place, it's very discouraging. No matter how hard I peddle, I never can catch up with that woman who is two feet in front of me. In the second place, I am always a little bothered by the sneaking conviction that my dear wife is a coward at heart. Why doesn't she have the faith to let me ride the front while she sits in the back?

I am still wiggling my toes and trying to reach a decision regarding this evening. It would be fun just to stay home and read a book. I started a new murder mystery last night, and I could probably finish it off quickly if I set my mind to it. On the other hand, it would be nice to go out to dinner and then to join friends for euchre. My nice deck of Braille cards is usually pretty close at hand. Please don't make any nasty remarks about the preacher using marked cards. I don't take unfair advantage of folks too often.

There's going to be a good basketball game on the radio tonight. That possibility offers me an interesting alternative. Please notice that I did not say that the game would be on TV. Even blind people can enjoy television for many things, but sports is not one of them. TV announcers always assume that you are watching the tube, and they sometimes allow their chatter to wander from the subject at hand. During a baseball game, for instance, the announcer can reminisce about the way it used to be while he and his brother were playing ball, while a home run, a triple and a stolen home plate can be transpiring on the field. A radio announcer never makes such a mistake. He knows that the listener is totally dependent upon his description. When it comes to sports, I am a radio man from the word go.

Come to think of it, radio is the very thing for tonight. In recent months I have become a Ham. KA9-RPN is my radio call, and I have spent many stimulating hours sending its greetings to other novice operators all over the continent. Being a minister has some advantages that no one would ordinarily think of. As a pastor, for instance, I can anchor my 120 foot long wire Ham antenna to the steeple of the nearby church. Who else in this world has an available radio tower that is forty-five feet up from the ground?

I am impressed by the many Hams who end their messages with the words, "God bless". Really, I am impressed by the quality of men and women whom I have met through the air waves. I am new in the business of Hamming, and going on the air tonight sounds pretty exciting. These are my plans until my wife calls in from the kitchen and wants to know if I care to be beaten in Scrabble. Them's fighting words.

My day is now coming to an end, and as I slip in under the covers I am reminded of a saying that is attributed to the late Helen Keller. Approached by an innocent who had almost no conception of what it is to be blind or for that matter deaf, Miss Keller was asked if she closed her eyes when she went to sleep. Helen Keller responded by declaring that she never stayed awake to find out.

The day that you and I have now shared has not been at all remarkable. As a matter of fact, you may have learned as much about ministry as you have about blindness. I keep telling folks that sightlessness is one of my lesser attributes. It is but a very small part of who I am.

No sensible person wants to be blind. As a matter of fact, no sane individual desires any of life's limiting maladies. The fact is, though, that blindness is nothing like the fearful spectors that are often associated with it. Plastic eyes cannot see in living color. The other side of the coin is that they cannot separate the blind person from the vitality that gives color to life. I hope that you have come to experience the leading edge of possibility as you have shared this day with me. I'd talk about it more, but I'm tired, and I want to go to bed.

I speculate about the mystery of me
And raise probing questions about what I am, who I am, and why I am.
I cannot comprehend the confluence of forces that shape me;
I am an unending riddle that baffles my introspection.
My searching mind shifts to take in those about me:
The girl on roller skates, the boy on a bike, the old man headed
towards the restaurant;
I consider the uniqueness of each and stand benumbed,
For if I don't understand me, how can I hope to appreciate them?
Yet I can talk to them, and they to me,
And in the conversation there is discovery;
For though the mantle of complexity always covers us,
In the process of searching there is the juice of life.

A Time To Talk Together

I am reminded of the seven-year-old who approached his mother one evening and asked her what sex is. He was rewarded by a nervous parental gulp and a half-hour discourse concerning birds, bees, cats, dogs, and other facts of life. The little boy shifted his weight from right foot to left and finally said, "Gee, mom, how am I going to put all this on the top line of that little card the teacher gave me?"

I suspect that it is commonplace for speakers and writers to deal with questions that are in their own heads, rather than those that may dwell in the minds of their listeners and readers. For this reason I have made a practice of ending each of my frequent public talks about blindness with an open session of questions and answers. When I first ask, "Are there questions?" there is usually an extended pause during which no one speaks. After the first few seconds there comes a tentative question, and then the floodgates of inquiry are open. Question time is often much longer than was my presentation itself. Quite apart from what I think they may want to hear, folks have a huge load of concerns that they are anxious to consider. I have often found that question time is the most profitable time that I can spend with a group.

How can I forget the evening in Warsaw, Indiana, when a young man asked me if I had a cane that went "beep beep?" He had seen a blind television detective with such a device, and he was sure that I would have one too. In the days of high technology such a cane may in fact be in production. Back at the time the question was asked of me, it most certainly was not. I'll never forget the boy's frustration, though, when he said, "Well, Longstreet (the TV detective) has one; why don't you?"

The fact is that I take all talk-back questions seriously. Quite often folks are asking about matters that they have never before had the chance to discuss. After all, not many people have a friendly neighborhood blind man whom they feel close enough to that they may approach him and say, "You know, I've always wondered about . . ."

In this chapter I want to reflect some of the questions that have been asked me the most often. I hope that they represent the wonderings that have been wandering through your mind as you have been reading this monologue. I wish that you could raise your inquiries personally, but since you can't, I'll do my best to anticipate your questions.

Do You Use A Guide Dog?

This is a question that comes up almost every time. It is born out of genuine personal interest and the sense of wondering joy that we have all had as we have seen man's best friend doing a wonderful job for many a sightless citizen. My answer is no.

I do not have a guide dog. I am sure that my miniature poodle would not qualify for such a title. Maybe at some future time when I enter retirement, I will desire a Seeing Eye friend. Right now, though, I'll settle for a cane and my poodle.

Let me explain myself this way. In the first place, I am a minister who does public relations work for God. It is my job to make friends and not to turn folks off. I know perfectly well that the law allows a guide dog to go almost everywhere, but the law is not the point. Can you imagine the feelings of Mrs. Jones who despises dog hair, or of Mrs. Smith who is comfortably situated with her nine cats if I should make a pastoral call with my very legal canine? I doubt if I would be invited back.

For me there is another wrinkle to the problem. Almost every day that I do calling an auto becomes a necessity. Either I need to visit the hospital that is eight miles away in Kokomo, or I want to stop at a nursing home that is about the same distance in the opposite direction. If I am just going door-to-door, I will find myself visiting folks who live way out in the country. It is to a guide dog's eternal credit that he has never tried to drive a car. What I am trying to say is that my pastoral work is inevitably tied to sighted human drivers. If I am out with such a person, I simply don't need a dog at the same time.

Incidentally, don't accept the myth that guide dogs are infallible. I love the tale told me by a blind friend who went with his pooch to a hobby show in Indianapolis. While the blind person sat at a display table demonstrating his hobbies, the faithful hound moved about the display hall. By the time that my blind friend was ready for lunch, his dog knew enough to bypass the lunch line and go straight to the kitchen. You can make a case that the pooch was pretty bright, but it's equally true that one blind person ended up where he hadn't intended to go.

Do Some Senses Improve As Others Decline?

This question reflects a wide-spread assumption that a blind person's ears, nose, and taste buds will be given amazing capacities strong enough to compensate for that person's loss of sight. Psychologically the idea is probably a subconscious attempt to explain away life's obvious inequalities. It does, in fact, reflect a half grain of truth, but the notion is really crazy and without any sense of reality.

Frankly the popular mythology of compensating senses furnishes blind folks (I suspect other handicapped persons, too) with a real and sneaky source of fun. It gives us one chance to laugh up our sleeves at the expense of everyone else.

Consider my friend Chet. Chet was president of our Butler University Tau Kappa Epsilon house a couple of years before I came on the scene. Chet was totally blind; he had been too close to an exploding hand grenade during the closing months of World War II. As president of our fraternity, Chet always sat at the head table during our evening meals.

Now let me introduce Mrs. B. She was our new housemother, and she was coming to spend her first evening with us. As the new mom, she also was to sit at the head table, right beside Chet, in fact.

Chet had heard the word that Mrs. B. was a bit nervous about sitting next to a blind person. He understood the situation. He also recognized the opportunity for a bit of fun. It only took minimal research for him to get the game going.

As soon as grace had been offered and all were seated, Chet commenced his act. He swung his head from side to side and began to sniff loudly. He finally turned directly towards the new house mother, continued to sniff, and declared that, "I smell red." With the sniffing going on, and the declarations of the smell of red getting louder and louder, Chet finally asked Mrs. B. if she were wearing a red dress. He had the poor woman totally convinced that his nose had gained such unique powers as to be able to determine color. It was a grand hoax.

How many times has an act like that been repeated? The humor of the handicapped certainly aids and abets credulous, popular mythology.

A moment ago I said that there was a half grain of reality to the notion of compensating senses. It is true that handicapped persons learn to make better use of their remaining powers. Take me, for instance. I certainly do not hear better than I did before I lost my sight. As a matter of fact, my hearing has slipped a bit in recent years and I have lost a certain amount of high frequency detection. The other side of the coin is that I probably use my ears better than I ever did before. I have learned to pay attention to the auditory signals that most people allow to go in one ear and out the other.

It is a January day as I write these words. The football-loving U.S. is waiting for the Super Bowl that is due to be played next Sunday. My imagination moves ahead and contains a picture of events that will transpire in many an American home.

The scene of my imagination is the television room. The wife enters and sweetly asks her husband if he will please carry out the trash. She is eager to get the house cleaned up, following the muss of the weekend. Hubby is parked in front of the set. It is first-and-goal and the score is tied. Not a single one of his spouse's words penetrates his brain.

"Darling, will you please carry the trash out?" The wife still receives no response at all. Now she is screaming: "Kindly take the trash out!" A moment later she stands between her husband and the set and declares, "You didn't hear a word I said!"

I wonder if you get the point. Nothing is wrong with hubby's ears. His wife's dulcet tones will register perfectly upon auditory nerve ends and will be properly transmitted to the ear drum and beyond. The point is that his attention will purposefully shut out the sounds that he doesn't want to hear. In a very profound sense, and even though his ears are in perfect working order, he will not have heard her.

Most of us live in a world of sensory information and simply shut out a great number of the sights, sounds, and smells that come to us. I can, for example, listen to the footsteps of a person walking down the hall in my church and tell with reasonable reliability whether the walker is a man or a woman. (A woman's steps tend to be shorter and quicker than a man's.) A sighted person would not need to use his ears in such a way. He can simply look and tell without question the sex of the one in the corridor.

The distinction that I am making may seem pretty subtle, but it is very important. A handicapped person's other senses do not improve; his or her use of them does. The ability to employ senses in an accelerated way has always been with people. It generally takes a handicap, though, to activate it and make it work. Blind men don't smell color, but their ability to make exceptional use of their remaining senses has written many a volume of popular mythology.

How Can I Best Help A Blind Person?

I am phrasing the question specifically in relation to the blind. Although I suspect that my answer could be applied to those with other handicapping conditions too, I dare not speak for them.

All people are different and no two blind persons are the same. I offer two tentative suggestions knowing that they make sense to me and my world of experience. I believe that they may encompass others too.

First, help a blind person and don't push him. In order to feel what I'm talking about, why don't you put on a blindfold for a minute and allow someone else to steer you about the building. You have the cloth tightly over your eyes, and you are totally dependent upon your friend for safe mobility. Now, try an experiment. See if you would rather have your guide take your arm and push you along, or if you would prefer to take his arm and follow. If you are the same sort of person that I am, you will have a total preference for the latter.

You and I don't like to be pushed. It is a scary business to be shoved in front of someone and to gamble that your guide will see the staircase or the roller skate in time to warn you of them. When you follow, on the other hand, you always have the subconscious knowledge that you are a free person who can start and stop at will. Even more important, you know that if you are holding your guide's arm, you will be walking slightly behind him and he, not you, will be the one to first meet the stair or skate.

The operative principle is that of asking how you may help. A sighted person's temptation is to rush in and do things for the helpless one. He must remember that it is his real task to assist and guide rather than to do and shove.

If you are to be with a blind person for an extended period of time, it would be good for you to find out about his specific abilities and needs. You can do this by watching carefully. You can also come right out and ask, "What special kinds of help do you need?" If the sightless person is at all adjusted to his situation, he will probably tell you.

As a side note, let me say that there are many tricky little aids and appliances that are made for blind persons. These are generally supplied at minimal cost by the American Foundation For The Blind in New York. If you have a blind person in your home or family, you will want to write for a catalogue. Watches, calculators, playing cards, thermometers, and countless other items that have been especially tailored for the needs of the sightless are readily available.

The second big answer that I would offer regarding the question at hand is to urge you to accept your friend's blindness and to help him do the same. Joe may be blind, but he is not deaf, speechless, and nuts. Treat him like a person, and don't worry about his lack of vision. Test him out to see how well he can joke and how much he is willing to say about being blind.

I recall that self-acceptance was my toughest job when I first lost my sight. I knew that I couldn't see, but I couldn't bring myself to use the word "blind." My inability to face up to my situation got me into some interesting special problems.

I recall a certain Friday afternoon during my freshman college year. My friends had all left school early, and I had to phone for a taxi to get home. I told the cab dispatcher where I would be and almost whispered the fact that I was "without sight." Had I said "blind," she might have gotten the message. She did not pass along my "lack of sight"communication, and the cab driver came and went without me. I found out later that he had come to the door of the room where I was and had stood right in front of me. When I didn't get up and come to him, and when no one else did either, he turned his back and left in a huff.

Then there was the day that I registered for the draft. The year was 1953, and draft registration was a very important business. Mom went with me as I made my obligatory trip to the draft board. She helped me fill in the form, and when we came to the question of special physical problems, I once again used the term "lack of sight." Do I need to tell you that the nicety of the language slipped past the gaze of a tired and frustrated civil service servant? When I got my draft card, I was stunned to discover that this blind man was registered as 1-A, fit for immediate service.

It was hard for me to learn to say the word "blind." Being able to say it, though, was a big part of getting hold of who I was.

Please remember what I said earlier about pushing. If a blind person doesn't want to admit that he's blind, it won't help to push. Some gentle guidance, though, can be awfully helpful.

Do People Ever Take Advantage of You Because You Can't See?

I am sure that there are times when they do. I am also sure that these times are pretty few and far between. As a matter of fact, I know that I have never been ripped off by someone who has intentionally given me bad change. Neither have I been mugged or robbed on the street. I have often joked and said that the same person who would mug you, might offer me a helping arm through the busy traffic. I guess that there is an essential decency in all of us. The image of vulnerability seems to evoke that decency. It has happened again and again.

I could tell a similar tale regarding folks who might act up behind my back, or in my case, in front of my plastic gaze. I am thinking, for example, of kids in Sunday School. I am sure that those whom I am teaching may seize the occasion of being unseen to send a few extra notes to one another. Generally, though, my sightlessness seems to put them on their best behavior.

I personally believe in trusting kids. If they think that I'm trying to watch out for them and catch them, they will enter into the game of one-upmanship with gusto. Short of mayhem, there is no way that an adult can win a contest like that. The other side of the coin is that kids will tend to rise to your level of expectation. A well-known oil company used to have an advertising phrase that went, "You expect more from Standard, and you get it." It's true; you expect more of folks, and you get it.

Did Your Blindness Have Any Effect Upon Your Going Into The Ministry?

Let me give a straightforward answer to this question. It is yes, no, and maybe. As a formative force in my life, my lack of sight surely made some contribution towards the making of each of my major decisions. There were, however, other forces at work around and within me.

Until my freshman year in college, I had held wild and energetic dreams about being a concert violinist. I had developed a profound admiration of Jascha Heifetz and dreamed of a time when I, too, could walk onto the concert stage with instrument in hand. My ambitions were not totally unfounded. I had studied the violin for about eight years and had developed a fair amount of skill with it. I was playing Mozart, Wieniawski, and a number of the other great and challenging composers.

Reality struck me with full force during my opening college year. My blindness was surely a part of it, for I had to face up to the truth that learning and memorizing music by ear is a pretty slow and tricky business. I have always had a good musical ear. I have been blessed with perfect pitch, which, in the simplest terms, means that I can listen to any musical note played on the piano and tell by hearing whether it is a C, a D, or an F-sharp. Even with perfect pitch, though, learning concert quality music by ear is rough going. I began to find my mind boggled by the thought of how much work it would take to develop a significant concert repertoire.

The other side of my newly-awakened reality would have struck me even if I had possessed 20/20 vision. It's awfully hard to make it to the concert stage and to walk in Heifetz's formidable shoes. For every aspiring person who makes the grade, there are thousands who don't. Perhaps I could liken my ambition to that of the kid who dreams of playing third base for the Yankees. There is the slightest chance that he will make it all the way to Yankee Stadium. The probability is, though, that if he does get to the stadium, he is more likely to be seated in the left field bleachers than to be standing astride the third base line. How can I know what might have been for me? I suspect that sooner or later the facts of economic and professional life would have caused me to lay my fiddle down.

In any event, realities started to press in on me, and I began to ask myself what I should be doing for employment and fulfillment during the majority of my lifetime. I thought, and talked to friends, and thought some more. I found myself dealing with two great questions.

What needs to be done in this world? This was my first question, and the answer wasn't very long in coming to me. It was early 1954; the Korean War had just ground to its conclusion, and the fear of the atom bomb was everywhere. Across the street from my house a neighbor was building a bomb shelter. Everyone was wondering if it would be worse to die in the original blast or to be trapped in a shelter with fearful, demented friends and neighbors who were fighting over the last drop of water and chunk of bread. I said to myself that if there is anything that the people of this world need it is the ability to live with one another in harmony. The need was obvious. It remains so to this day.

What special talents and abilities do I have? This second inquiry wasn't hard to answer either. I certainly could talk. My loving uncle had always accused mom of having vaccinated me with a talking machine needle. Likewise, I seemed to have a natural ability to relate to people and their problems.

I have already told you about my fraternity house experiences with guys who would spill out their hearts and hurts to me. I didn't know why they were doing it, but it was perfectly obvious to me that they were. My skills and natural abilities (contemporary clergymen use the term "gifts and graces") seem to be clearly focused towards people-helping, both in terms of speaking and counseling.

Accept for a moment the fact that I had grown up in the Church, and then take a pencil and trace the pattern of the world's need and of my perceived abilities. If you are as I was, you find yourself looking at a cross. The need of this world for peace and my own ability to speak and relate seemed to intersect at a point which was clearly marked "ministry." Undoubtedly, the fact that both of my grandfathers had been Evangelical United Brethren pastors played a certain part in my thinking. Basically, though, the decision was my own.

I have not written on my "Christian call" in the sense that God spoke from heaven, or that a divinely sent sign appeared in the clouds above my head. If such a sign should have manifested itself in the clouds, I wouldn't have been able to see it anyhow. To me God has never spoken or acted in such dramatic ways. I have always found that His Spirit moves deep within the frame of my thoughts and experiences. I am seldom able to separate God's voice from the sounds of my thoughts and those of my world. I am convinced that the "call" did come to me, though, and that God did express His desires for me within the spectrum of my searching intelligence. I have never seriously doubted the validity of His call or of my decision.

In previous pages I have told you of the unique ministerial strengths with which my lack of sight has endowed me. My blindness is, after all, a part of who I am. The totality of me (blindness, baldness, and all) was called into the ministry. My blindness is, then, part of the personal package.

Rev. Karstedt, How Do You Prepare A Sermon?

Over seventeen years have passed since this question was asked of me by a lady in a Lebanon, Indiana, church. I suppose that I was being a bit of a wise guy when I answered it. I pulled at my chin and said, "How do I prepare a sermon? How does anyone prepare a sermon? Ask your minister where his sermon ideas come from; I'll bet that he and I are about the same."

For a few moments I couldn't understand why my remarks broke our entire audience up into torrents of laughter. I stood confused until a lady in the front row was nice enough to tell me that the minister's wife was the one who had posed the question.

I may have been a little flippant with my original answer, but I think that I would still want to stand by it. I have already told you about the mechanics that I employ in making a sermon ready for presentation. Some sighted pastors use the same mechanics that I do. Most ministers use pencil and paper in some way that is foreign to me. I stress now that such procedures are only matters of mechanics. The question of really preparing a sermon is a profound one. I often say that creating a sermon is a little like having a baby. Since my experience at having babies is somewhat limited, I must beg for your indulgence as I explain what I mean.

At the beginning of every sermon, there must be the magical moment of conception. Two intersecting forces must meet and be touched by the Spirit of God. The requisite forces are those of life experience and of Biblical truth. Somehow, somewhere, a need in the world and a truth revealed in Scripture must unite within the mind, soul, and imagination of a preaching pastor. No sermon of real worth can take form unless these forces have merged and have become a sermon idea.

How does a pastor cause such a time of conception to take place? He doesn't force it to happen; he simply allows the event. It is imperative that the minister should read the Scriptures regularly and faithfully. He must constantly study the Word and allow it to speak to him. On the other hand, the vital pastor must consult life everywhere he goes. Newspapers, works of fiction, television dramas . . . the list goes on and on. A pastor needs to feel and resonate with the aches and aspirations of his world. His mind, soul, and imagination can then become the arena where need and truth can meet. When it happens, the moment is marvelous.

I have always been glad that I do not have to punch a time clock. There is not a single person in my congregation who could comprehend my working hours. How can I explain that some of my deepest inspirations strike me when I am in the bathroom? (Please, no remarks about my sermons having gone to pot or being all wet!) The fact remains, though, that inspiration strikes at odd times. It usually comes when I am relaxed and the ideas of my studying and experiencing can move freely within me. I may wake up at 4:00 a.m. and find myself excited by the power of a great idea. It is what I call sermonic conception. God's inspiring spirit doesn't seem to punch a time clock either.

I will move quickly through the rest of the process. After conception there must be gestation. There simply needs to be time for the idea to grow and develop. I often encourage gestation by discussing my ideas with persons with whom I share lunch. The time required for gestation can be extended or shrunk. The process is, however, imperative.

After gestation, there comes the time for labor. No minister can do without it. I must go to my study, hammer out my thoughts, and find the words that I need to express them. After labor, there comes delivery.

I know that many contemporary experts in childbirth are now talking about the value of a warm, welcoming environment for a newborn child. The same is true for a sermon. It is very hard to preach to a frigid and rigid congregation. Believe me when I write that the warmth and acceptance of a congregation is requisite to the health and well-being of the freshly delivered sermon. You, the listener, are part of the process too. Please remember this always.

Sometimes we want to make much too much of so-called handicapping conditions. I think that most preachers would say "amen" to the preceding remarks about sermon development. It is very dangerous to suppose that blind persons think in ways that are strange to other folks. I have dealt with this matter of sermon creation in order to illustrate the fact that, handicapped or not, we are very much the same.

Are You Ever Discouraged And Depressed?

Of course I am; who isn't? Life has its ups and downs for all of us. Although we each operate on a different emotional cycle, periodic moments of depression are natural and necessary.

May I go on to note that the question in hand usually implies much more than it says. Some folks have images of blind persons who spend their days stumbling through their world of darkness and cursing the fate that put them in such a state. I tend to be a person with a happy public countenance. I genuinely like people, and I am usually smiling and laughing when I am with others. The image of a grumbling blind man and the reality of a smiling Ralph don't fit together very well, and folks often wonder what I am like when they aren't around.

Cursing the darkness has never been a big thing for me. I lost my sight when I was relatively young and flexible. Although I had plenty of down moments back then, I managed to bounce back to emotional equilibrium rather easily. Being without sight is now a simple fact of life to me. I accept it, live with it, and seldom philosophize and mutter about it.

If I am going to be depressed about something, I will probably enter my purple mood because of a more current matter. If something has gone wrong at the church, if my wife and I have had a few sharp words, or if the rains come on an afternoon when I am dead tired and need a good bike ride, then, I am likely to sink into the temporary doldrums.

I said a moment ago that times of depression are very natural. Let me go on to declare that they are not at all faithless. Christian people often find themselves confused because of emotions that seem to be out of keeping with their faith. They wonder if it is really appropriate for a faithful one to fear the future and to question if it is really true that "in everything God works for good with those who love him . . ." (Romans 8:28, R.S.V.) They feel guilty about tears shed at a graveside, for they remember their expressed faith in the resurrection. They cannot accept their flashes of rage and anger, because they feel as though they should model the life of one who asked us to love one another always. Emotional acceptance can sometimes be a very tricky matter, and heavy guilt for unwanted emotions is often heaped upon the unwanted feelings themselves.

Perhaps it is time for us to remember the totality of Jesus' life. Can we recollect the time when He stood beside a tomb in Bethany and wept? Are we able to recall the bitter tears that He shed in the garden of Gethsemane? What of His heart-wrenching cry from the cross: "My God, my God, why hast thou forsaken me?" (Matthew 27:46, R.S.V.) Isn't it clear that Jesus had His down times too?

Let's look for a thoughtful moment at the deep meanings of faith and of God's being with us in the midst of our lives. I am reminded of the father who came to Christ with the request that He should heal an epileptic son. "Heal him if you can," the father said. "If I can?" Jesus replied. "Don't you believe that with God all things are possible?" "I believe," cried the distraught father; "Help my unbelief!" (Mark 9:22-24, paraphrased)

Belief is always counterbalanced by doubt. Belief is not knowledge; it is doubt-shrouded expectancy and trust. The Biblical father whom I quoted a moment ago is one of my patron saints. He helps me to understand the penetrating depth of faith.

The point is that God has never promised to carry us to mountain tops of unending joy and delight. His word to us is much more gutty and real. He has told us that He will be with us in the dark valleys. The psalmist understood the matter perfectly when he wrote: "Even though I walk through the valley of the shadow of death, I fear no evil; for thou art with me . . ." (Psalms 23:4, R.S.V.)

God's help for us does not take us from the realities of this life. Rather, it makes it possible for us to live. In the midst of joys and sorrows, victories and defeats, moments of elation and times of utter despair, God is with us. As long as they come at appropriate times, we need not be afraid of our natural emotions. For us to walk in the dark valley, daring to believe that God will bring us out of the depths of pain and despair that envelop us, is far more practical and faithful than for us to pretend that the valley doesn't exist. We need not feel confused and guilty when we find its shadows drawn tight about us.

Forgive me for using a simple question as an excuse to do a lot of preaching. Let me be straightforward. Yes, I have my low times. No, I'm not ashamed of them. They are, for me, usually more immediate than is my loss of sight. I find my down times to be occasions when my faith is enlarged and strengthened.

I have tried to deal honestly and thoughtfully with the profound questions that have been put to me during the years. Of course, there have been other inquiries too. Folks ask me how I count money, how I tell time, and how I know what color my shirt and tie are. Would you take my word for it that these are simple problems with easy solutions? I count money carefully, use my fingers and my Braille watch to tell time, and usually trust Mary Evelyn to match up my shirts and ties. The system normally works very well. When all else fails I have my beloved pooch. Mr. French growled at me the other morning when I picked up a brown sweater to wear along with my red tie. He has doggone good taste.

I spoke to one who has never seen, and remarked that the sky is blue.
" 'Blue,' " he said; "tell me what 'blue' is."
"Why blue is like the summer lake, like my daughter's eyes; 'blue'
    is blue."
He could not comprehend; to him my words were senseless noises.
    How often is it so when we talk together?
    How often do I use words that have no meaning to you?
    How can I know that my interpretation is the same as yours?
    Do we live in a cacophonous world of senseless syllables?
When I say "dog," I wonder if you have the image of a poodle,
Or if I say "poodle," if you see him as being black?
And if we cannot talk with satisfaction about a dog,
How can we ever speak together of more complicated matters?
    So it is that you and I converse,
    With each trying to express himself more than to be understood,
    And our voices project a flood of verbal images;
    Are we communicating or simply complicating our human
        problem?
Let us make a start at understanding
By listening with intensity greater than that with which we speak
And let us remember the power of a smile
Whose clarity is more profound than that of any spoken language.

Enlargements

Enlargements are sometimes very beautiful and satisfying. On the other hand, the process of blowing an image or idea up to a size beyond its own frequently results in distortion and confusion. Knowing whether enlargement can be successfully undertaken sometimes demands a level of wisdom that is nearly superhuman.

I think of a marvelous picture that sits upon the dresser in our bedroom. My daughter took it a couple of years ago while we were in Cairo, Egypt. The photo was taken while we were in a felucca that was sailing the Nile and being driven by a moderate breeze. It shows a brilliant golden sunset that silhouettes the skyline of old Cairo and casts reflections upon the rippling waters of the river. The shot was taken in 35 mm. Beth had the tiny image enlarged and presented us the eight by ten as a treasured Christmas gift. It is wonderful.

Magnification, however, sometimes fails to tell the complete story. Try taking a cup full of ocean water and imaginatively magnifying it a billion, billion times. The wetness and saltiness of the great Atlantic would be contained in our magnification. Somehow, though, we would fail to feel the surf on our skin, and we would miss the thunderings and rumblings of seething seas and ocean depths. Such an enterprise in enlargement would denude the sea of its oceanness.

As I have been writing these chapters and pages, I have constantly questioned myself about the possibility of enlarging and transposing my ideas and observations into an extended world of experience. Can the problems and peculiar strengths that I have known as a blind person be supposed to belong to other blind persons too? What of the deaf or the retarded? Can my thoughts be applied to the limiting factors (the handicaps) that each one of us possesses? I have been tempted to use my own world of experience as a microcosm of the human venture. I know that I must hedge my temptations, for distortions and consequent half-truth are possible, if not likely, results of the enlarging process.

It is, for example, very easy for me to move from my personal case study and to jump to the conclusion that all handicapped persons can carve out satisfying and worthwhile lives for themselves. I can even expand upon my belief that handicapping forces may be levers of possibility for them. There may be right in such an expansive thought, but I must be very careful. What right have I to speak to the quadriplegic or to the one who is severely retarded? I must only offer my own reflections as an example of one person's experience. Perhaps my words will provide a model of possibility for someone else. I would like to think that they can.

The fact is that society in general does plenty of enlarging in reference to personal weakness. Society tends to take any handicapping and limiting condition and to blow it far out of proportion.

How often have Mary Evelyn and I taken our seats at a restaurant and been approached by a condescending waitress who asks Mary Evelyn if "he likes cream in his coffee." It is as though she sees my blindness and immediately assumes that I must be deaf, mute, and stupid as well.

The business of magnifying handicaps goes clear back to Bible days. Let's think for a moment about a fascinating account that appears in the first chapter of Luke's gospel. Zechariah, as Luke tells the tale, goes into the temple to offer burnt incense to God. While there he is confronted by the angel Gabriel, who tells him that he and his wife Elizabeth are going to have a baby. Zechariah says, "You're kidding!" Gabriel replies that because of his disbelief, Zechariah will be unable to speak until the baby is born. (Luke 1:20)

Now here comes the rest of the story. In nine months or so, Elizabeth and her now mute husband have their baby. After the child is born, the neighbors gather around and say, "What are you going to name him?" When Elizabeth replies with the name "John," the neighbors say, "Why John? There's no one by the name of John in your family." Elizabeth insists that the new boy should be called John.

Now the neighbors turn to Zechariah. What do they do? They "make signs" to him asking what the child's name shall be. (Luke 1:62) Let me ask you: why should they make signs? Is poor Zechariah mute or is he deaf? Either Luke has misled us in telling all about Zechariah's problem, or the neighbors are doing something that makes no sense at all. They have treated Zechariah as though he were "deaf and dumb." What about the word, "dumb?" Doesn't it extend the handicap of muteness into the range of mental inferiority? How commonplace it is for us to enlarge the handicaps of those about us.

I have often observed this phenomenon and have wondered why we do such things. I speculate that it represents a subconscious attempt to assure ourselves that we aren't at all like the poor person who is before us. If I can enlarge my image of Joe's handicap, I can convince myself that I am not at all like he is. Joe becomes some sort of freak in my mind. I remain a perfectly normal human being.

How hard it is for us to recognize our own humanity. How hard it is for us to face up to the fact that we are each vulnerable, limited, handicapped in a sense. We are like Zechariah, like Joe, like Ralph.

A fellow pastor tells me of an experience that came to him during his day as chaplain for our state legislature. Soon after his mid-morning arrival at the state house, Rev. C. was given the grand guided tour. He was ushered through the meeting halls of both house and senate and was shown the chambers where the supreme court sits in its judgment of lofty matters. As he was exposed to state house, legislators, and television news personnel, Rev. C. was duly impressed. The pastor was introduced to our lieutenant governor about ten minutes before the official session was to commence with the chaplain's prayer. It seemed that both men were, at that moment, struck by the same powerful need, for they found themselves marching together to the men's room and standing side by side before the plumbing. Although he certainly knew better, Rev. C. was subconsciously surprised to discover that the lieutenant governor did it too.

Rev. C.'s impressions reflect the attitudes of many of us. We find ourselves so awed by the grandeur and power of office and position that we lose sight of our leaders' basic humanity. We are brought up short when we find ourselves standing at the same urinal with the lieutenant governor.

Perhaps the issue is that we want our leaders to be supermen. We want to believe that they are infinitely stronger, wiser, and more noble than we are. How could we sleep at night if we knew that those thousands of persons who, in one way or another, have their fingers on the nuclear trigger are frail, fallible, insecure, tempestuous persons just like ourselves? I honestly believe that it is our unreal and artificially lofty view of our national leaders that allows us to take part in the current arms acceleration. If we could see the souls of the men who stand behind our bombs, ships, planes, and guns, we would rip those instruments of destruction out of their hands immediately.

Please understand that I am not entering into a vendetta of character assassination. Our leaders and military personnel are, for the most part, decent and well-meaning people. The problem is that they are people — finite, fallible, emotion-ridden, limited people. They are like you and me, like Zechariah, like Joe, like Ralph.

But we want our leaders to be supermen. It is therefore extraordinarily hard for us to accept their humanity. Catch the president in a half-truth; discover a senator involved in an act of moral indiscretion; listen in to hear what the preacher says when he hits his thumb with the hammer — such acts seem unpardonable. We do not want to believe that our leaders are as frail and vulnerable as we are. We will not believe it. If we find a flawed leader, we'll throw the rascal out and fill his place with someone else. Coming face to face with our own vulnerability is too painful to endure.

There is a tricky little piece of partial logic that supports us as we search for perfection among those with whom we trust our lives. I call this twist of logic the "weakest-link syndrome." Every one of us has been brought up knowing the adage that a chain is no stronger than its weakest link. Although I'm no whiz in matters mechanical, I assume that the saying is true in so far as chains are concerned. The problem is that we want to apply "chain logic" to people. Such an application just doesn't work.

Here's the way we do it. We say that a chain is no stronger than its weakest link; a person is no better than his weakest quality. If we can discover a flaw in a person, then we know what's the matter with him or her, and we can lay that person aside and go look for another leader. It sounds right, doesn't it? There is just one problem; we are all flawed. Every last one of us has some sort of weak link in his or her personal makeup.

"Weak link" thinking tends to magnify limitations and to pay little regard to strength. It tends to transform a blind man into a person who is unable to hear, speak, and think as well. It turns a presidential misstatement into an act of incompetency, and a congressman's indiscretion into a manifestation of depravity. It even turns the minister who mutters a momentary oath into a heretic or a pagan.

Surely we need to eliminate our tendencies for character exaggeration regarding our national and spiritual leaders. When we see these persons as limited humans, we will at the same time reduce the amount of power that we place in finite hands and become more accepting of the human factor that is part of all our personhood.

In an earlier page I wrote that my blindness sometimes forces my parishioners to face up to their own humanity. We need the obviously handicapped persons in our midst. They force us to deal responsibly with the limited strengths and qualities of us each.

A few weeks ago I found myself sharing breakfast with a man who has spent many professional years directing a workshop for the retarded. He told me that he sometimes wants to throw up his hands and give up on the whole effort of helping retarded persons to have an accepted place in our society. "It's impossible," he said. "What you say about the handicapped having a rightful place among us sounds nice, but it just isn't realistic."

As we continued to talk a waitress stepped to our table and began to refill our coffee cups. When she turned away my companion remarked that a retarded person could be doing that job, but that society wouldn't let such a thing happen. "Can you imagine retarded people serving as waiters and waitresses in fine restaurants?" he asked. "Customers would never return if such persons were serving them."

In my heart I had to agree that my breakfast companion was absolutely correct. After we parted I had a second thought. People like us are the ones that keep my friend's retarded workers from serving our tables. Although a great number of retarded persons might not be able to handle such responsibilities, many of them are perfectly able to do the job. You and I, not they, are the ones who hold back their ability to accomplish.

In an earlier chapter I referred to an excellent book, *The Making Of Blind Men*. The book addresses the same issue that I am now endeavoring to expand. Society "makes" people handicapped when it enlarges and builds upon the idea of the handicap rather than that of the strengths that any individual may have. Furthermore, if society spends enough time and effort telling someone that he or she can't do something, the probability is that such a person will never do it. Our patterns of thought and action are constricting lives and binding them with the chains of handicap, rather than helping limited persons to slip free from their bonds and to discover how to live fruitfully and freely within the spectrum of their strengths.

May I return for one last moment to the thought that we are all handicapped? We are all limited by some physical factor or cultural force. It may be a weakness of body, a matter of skin coloration, a personality trait, a problem of family history, or a difficulty in economics. Society will be inclined to be condescending to us and our limitations. It will say: "He's not doing badly for a blind man, or for a black, or for one who is somewhat retarded, or for a person who was brought up in the slums." No matter what I write in these pages, society's ways of thinking and acting are not likely to change quickly. The person who wants to break free from the chains of expected failure that are laid upon him will have to do it for himself. We each have strengths and possibilities within us. Curiously, our strengths are often the consequent forces that rise from our limitations.

In my blindness I find unique ability to minister to others. Who can help an alcoholic to kick the habit better than one who is a personal prisoner of alcohol himself? The fear-ridden person whose knees knock as he stands up to speak is passing through such an obvious struggle that all listen to him with heightened attention. The story goes on and on.

In this chapter I have been making some tentative enlargements upon the understandings that have come to me as I have observed and lived life. I know that these enlargements cannot be applied to all persons. I suspect, though, that they are applicable to most of us. For too long a time we have held unrealistic views of ourselves and our leaders. We need to be able to pay less attention to our weaknesses, place greater emphasis upon our strengths, and to have expectations for others that are commensurate with their respective frailties and abilities. As I look out from plastic eyes, that's the way I see it.

Now He steps into the resurrection garden
And views the world through Easter eyes.
    The beauty of new beginnings stands before His gaze,
    For sunlight flashes upon dew-glazed grass,
    And flowers dance before the urging of the morning breeze.
    Stirred by the freshness, He smiles in contentment.
And yet there is more that moves before His awareness,
For He looks upon disbelieving Mary, who does not recognize Him,
And His gaze shifts to consider Jerusalem's great walls
Which will soon be thrown down by the hands of warring men.
    It is a sad smile that is written on His face,
    For He sees that we, too, must face our Calvarys.
    And that the frustration of hurt and loss
    Must be our experience before, at last, we come ourselves to
        the garden.

Easter Epilogue

A single biker tops the crest of the hill and commences the long downgrade run to the lake. Other riders quickly come into view as in pairs and trios they enter into the wild descent. Our tandem is in the midst of the group, and Mary Evelyn shifts our dual derailleurs so as to put us in our highest gear. We pump hard and generate breakneck speeds to maintain our place in the midst of the pack.

We have been riding together for most of a week. There are twenty or so junior high boys and girls and a half dozen pedaling counselors. Up until now we have been well-disciplined and have ridden in groups of five or six young people and one counselor, but now we are on our last leg, and discipline has been thrown to the four winds. We are pedaling furiously as we swing through the tight turn and enter our northern Indiana campground. "Ride to the lake!" I scream. "Don't stop at the lodge!"

Red-faced, sweating, and happy, we pull up by the lakeside, dismount, lean our bikes against nearby trees, and collapse on the grassy lawn which leads out to the shore. I am handed a loaf of French bread. I break it and begin to talk to the kids.

Before going further, let me tell you about the day's riding that is now coming to an end. We have been involved in what we call a "Life of Christ" bike ride. It began early in the morning when we rode from our camp and made our first stop at the Shafer's barn. Our kids trooped into the barn where one of the group led us all in a two-minute devotion centered on the theme that Jesus was born in a stable. The devotion was closed as we sang "Silent Night." Some of us had a hard time keeping straight faces when an old horse standing in a stall right beside us stuck out his head and whinnied in accompaniment to our music. Somehow, "Mr. Ed," as the kids called him, made our remembrance of the nativity seem ever so real.

Our day continued as we made other stops, each of which helped us to remember an event in the life of Christ. By a small creek we were reminded of His baptism; at a lakeside we recollected the way He called His disciples. A hilltop provided us opportunity to celebrate the Sermon On the Mount; and when we stopped for lunch, we had an ideal chance to recollect the feeding of the five thousand. Just before you joined us, as we commenced our last dash back to camp, we had paused at a small cemetery and had been reminded of Jesus' death and burial.

Now, with a piece of bread in hand, I am talking to the campers. I remind them of the Sunday after Christ's death when two of His dejected disciples were walking a lonely road and making their way towards Emmaus. Their eyes were focused on the clouds of dust that were being stirred up by their dragging sandals; their spirits were equally downcast. When the risen Christ joined them and began to talk with them, Cleopas and his friend did not recognize Jesus.

The trio spoke at length concerning the tragic events of the weekend. They remembered Jesus' lonely and painful death, and Cleopas groaned as he told the "stranger" that Jesus' body was now missing from the grave and that it must be supposed that the body had been stolen. The conversation continued until the small group entered Emmaus and the two friends invited their traveling guest to join them for supper.

"It was then," I remind our young people as I lift up the loaf of bread, "as Jesus broke the bread and gave thanks for the meal, that Cleopas and his friend recognized Him. It was in this simple event that they discovered Him in their company."

It is a beautiful and very important story. I want our young bikers to remember it, and I must remind myself of it again and again. At the end of many long and lonely roads, when we are sweaty, dirty, and bone-tired, when it seems as though we have gone as far as we can go and have taken as much as we are able to take, the most simple of circumstances can remind us that He is with us and that He has been traveling in our midst all the time.

This book has not been written as a "Christian" enterprise. My real focus, as I have typed out these pages, has been that of describing life as I see it through the unique perspective of a pair of plastic eyes. The fact is, though, that I am a Christian and a minister. It is quite impossible for me to speak of the life that I live and know without reflecting, and indeed, basing much of my understanding, upon my our stance of faith. God is with us. He is present to give us purpose and strength in the most difficult of our experiences. I believe this fact firmly and would write it now as a benedictory thought.

We were on the Greek island of Chios. We were to have used this spot as a land-base from which we would have ferried into Turkey. Along with a strong September wind, heavy seas had arisen, however, and our ferry had not been allowed out of harbor. Our tour guide was giving us a conducted journey about the island and was allowing us to visit villages that are seldom entered by wandering Americans.

I have long since forgotten the name of the town that we came to in the early afternoon. Along with our fellow travelers, my wife and I climbed out of the bus and began to walk towards the center of the village. Mary Evelyn suddenly felt a tug upon her arm. We looked up into the smiling face of a local citizen, who motioned for us to follow him and who spoke to us in rapid Greek that was, to our hearing, quite unintelligible.

For a moment or so we wondered if we should accompany this total stranger. His smiling face carried the day and our decision, and we began to walk with him through the narrow streets of the town. We passed through the business block and began to make our way out towards the town wall that was on the far side of the community. As we trudged on, our friendly guide continued to motion for us to go with him and to "jabber" at us in Greek. We finally came to a very narrow alley which ran close to the town wall; our guide entered it, once again indicating that we should accompany him. With mounting misgivings we continued to follow.

Our willingness to stay with this beckoning stranger nearly came to an end when he gestured for us to go ahead of him through a narrow door that led from our alley. We had instant visions of being mugged, robbed, and worse. By this time, though, we were alone and pretty well committed. We stepped through the shadowed entry and found ourselves in an ancient Greek Orthodox Church.

The church is a treasure of faith and beauty. Because of its remote location, it is almost never beheld by Americans. Our guide pointed to its ceiling above us and said, "Christos, Pantokrator!" We knew and understood those words, for we had heard them before. They mean, "Christ, the risen and reigning Lord." Above our heads we saw, painted upon the ceiling, the likeness of the triumphant Christ and the host of heaven. We were thrilled by the beauty of the place and the meaning of the moment.

I have often thought about our strange visit to this obscure church of Chios. It has taken on the power of a parable for my life. I had to travel through dark alleys and found it necessary to draw upon an extra measure of courage before I was able to stand in the unexpected sanctuary. More than this, I had discovered the Easter church only because I was able to trust a guide whom I did not know. With these thoughts I end my Easter Epilogue and our entire visit together. I know that shadowed pathways and uncertain futures await us each. I firmly believe that it is when we pass through the darkness faithfully that we are the most likely to be surprised by our encounters with the living and loving Son of God. That's the way life is as I see it.